IT WAS FOR YOU

Lenten Sermons
by
Lutheran Pastors

AUGUSTANA BOOK CONCERN
ROCK ISLAND, ILLINOIS

AUGUSTANA BOOK CONCERN
Printers and Binders
ROCK ISLAND, ILLINOIS
1939

Foreword

During the Lenten season of 1939, Lutherans of Chicago united in sponsoring midday religious services in the heart of the city. It was the first time such a series of daily devotions had been arranged covering all the weeks in Lent.

This book contains all the sermons preached at these services. It is put out with the thought that these messages, after having been given to large local audiences and sent broadcast over the air in consecrated witnessing for Christ, still have in them that spirit and power which deepens devotion and builds stronger the faith of Christian men and women in Christ crucified and risen.

In gratitude to the eighteen pastors elsewhere named who gave their services and with whose courteous consent these Lenten sermons are issued, the publishers send this volume forth to carry their ministry into still another field where it may bear fruit—that of Christian literature.

JOSEPH SIMONSON.

Contents

6

The Supremacy of Christ

WALTER H. TRAUB

THE SUPREMACY OF CHRIST

*The kingdom of heaven is like unto a merchant man,
seeking goodly pearls:*
*Who, when he had found one pearl of great price, went
and sold all that he had, and bought it.* Matthew 13. 45–46.

THE lesson of the text is directed to people
who have learned to value good things. The
merchant sought for "goodly pearls." The church
of today is set in the midst of such people. Our
civilized, not to say Christianized, communities
are constant reminders of the fact that there are
multitudes of people who prize the fruits of
knowledge, the refinements of wealth, and the
blessings of democratic institutions. And it is to
such that the Christian church must ever insist
upon the importance of religion. Over against all
goodly pearls it must place the one pearl of sur-
passing worth. Contemporary life is a running
commentary on the truth that it is possible to
possess "goodly pearls," while missing the pearl
of pearls, the kingdom of God, without which all
other things are "of nothing worth."

In the first place, there is no essential connection between prosperity and moral and religious
character. It seems, generally, to be taken for
granted that so long as a man or a nation pros-
pers, all is well. A common answer in this coun-

try to the question, "Is the world growing better?" might run something like this: "Of course it is. Look at the material progress. We have the highest standard of living of any country in the world and of any period in history. Look at the steam engine, the telegraph, the radio, the airplane. Of course we are growing better." It does not seem to occur to us to consider whether the moral and ethical values are keeping pace with material progress. We do not stop to weigh the political, social, and ethical consequences of this well-being.

This identifying of prosperity with religion seems to be the result of a crude conception of the Old Testament idea—"Obey God, and you will prosper." But the history of the Bible does not allow us to assume that righteousness invariably goes with success. In a number of cases it shows the opposite to be true. Saul's good fortune in being raised to a throne did not improve his character. And a worm was already eating at the heart of the nation when it was at the height of national glory in the reign of Solomon. The lessons of the Bible are the lessons of history and experience. Nations have begun to die when their material resources were at the zenith. And all of us have known men who did not become better when they became richer. They died, like Hamlet's father, "full of bread."

We are not among those who cry down legitimate wealth. We would not go to the Master with the covetous clamor, "Speak to my brother, that he divide with me." In view of Christ's spirit and teaching, there is much in American life and enterprise which would have His admiration and approval. But that unclouded vision and uncanny insight of His would see something more. He would see that men are endeavoring to do that which He said could not be done, namely, "Worship God and mammon." He would see, further, one of the worst forms of moral obliquity that can pervade a people—a fear of failing so great that men stoop to anything to win.

Let us confess it. Commercialism threatens the fineness of our social fabric. Our novels tell it, and our streets, our pleasures and our politics, aye, and our pulpits. Life does consist in the abundance of things which we possess. Creation is loved more than the Creator. Let us confess, also, that in the minds of many the worst thing that could happen is failure. We honor riches without a soul more than we do a soul without riches. Men dread failure more than dishonor.

We must insist upon righteousness first, no matter if the cost be poverty and failure. In the interests of truth, let us emphasize that sin is the only failure. Sin means "missing the mark"; and lack of God's peace is the only poverty. God does not ask us to be prosperous, but to be true. If, being true, "all these things" are added, they will be all the sweeter, but if not, we can emulate the sublime spirit which said,

"It is not in man to command success,
  But we'll do more, Sempronius, we'll deserve it."

In the second place, there is no essential connection between education and moral and religious character. Education is a word to conjure with in America. And it is plainly seen why this should be so in a democracy. It would be easy to pile argument upon argument revealing the awful progeny of ignorance. We are told that in a certain penal institution 90% of the inmates never went to college, a large percentage did not go through high school and quite a number went no higher than the fourth grade. But figures are deceiving. They fail to note that the educated classes are able to avail themselves of powerful counsel out of the reach of the poor. And they do not take into account the fact that the few educated men who are serving time are a greater menace to society than the great mass of the ignorant. Horace Mann once said, "One educated scoundrel is more dangerous to a community than a score of ignorant scoundrels."

Unguided ignorance is a terrible thing. It is a blind giant. When the hordes of Alaric and Attila overran Europe, trampling the fair fruit of civilization into the dust, ignorance revealed what it was capable of doing. But unguided education, too, may become a curse of towering enormity. After the appalling spectacle of highly educated peoples running amuck in that same Europe in the most disastrous war of history, one may well ask whether, by education alone, there is not danger of producing a Frankenstein that will destroy us. You remember how a great chemist, in Mrs. Shelley's romance, built a man, adding bone to bone, laid sinews and flesh upon it, and galvanized it into life. But what a life! The monster went about committing atrocious crimes, and finally inflicted the most dreadful retribution upon his creator.

Carlyle, standing before the portraits of Goethe and Dante, was asked to name the difference reflected from the faces of the two. He replied in one word: "God." Is not this difference fundamental? Jesus divided men into the regenerate and unregenerate. We have come to divide them into the ignorant and educated. To hear some talk, you would suppose that the only test for entrance into heaven will be a literacy test. But the Master holds to the truth that a man may be educated and not be alive to moral and spiritual issues. Competent witnesses say that he is right. In the time of the German struggle, Wordsworth wrote that the educated were inactive and supine. Wendell Phillips, in an address to the Phi Beta Kappa Society, scourged the educated classes of America for their indifference during the slavery crisis. And Theodore Roosevelt in his book, *American Ideals,* rings the changes on the lack of ideals and moral stamina among the college men of his day. Educated themselves, these men would be the first to allow the numerous and notable exceptions. But William E. Gladstone, a man of wealth and university training, in a survey of his own day, said: "In almost every one of the great political controversies of the last fifty years, whether they affected the franchise or commerce or religion, the leisure class, the titled class, and the educated class, have been in the wrong."

The mind, too, has its Pharisees. Pharisees who tithe the mint and anise and cummin of technical knowledge, but omit the weightier matters of truth. Pharisees who make clean the outside of the cup and the platter, but show no interest about the inside. Pharisees who are like unto whited sepulchres, which indeed appear refined aid cultured outwardly, but are within full of dead men's bones.

Hazlitt reports a statement Charles Lamb made to a group of literary men: "If Shakespeare was to come into the room, we should all rise up to meet him; but if Christ was to come into it, we should all fall down and try to kiss the hem if His garment." He further states that immediately the company rose up to go as a lady present seemed to get uneasy at the turn the conversation had taken. We may believe that there are still some who would be uneasy to hear Christ praised above their beloved idol, but it ought to make us uneasy only when He is praised less. "The soul of all improvement is the improvement of the soul."

In the third place, there is no essential connection between nationality and moral and religious character. Real patriotism, which consists in the free giving of self for the good of all, is the passion which burned with such a pure flame in those rememberable yesterdays of our history.

But that is a different thing from the arrogant chauvinism which Dr. Johnson called, "The last refuge of a scoundrel." Says Dr. Nicholas Murray Butler, "A form of patriotism has been developed all over the world which finds in the nation itself the highest human end."

America must set its face strongly against this godless nationalism. Nationalism is the pride of place and the lust for power; patriotism is the passion for service and the sense of mission. Nationalism believes in the odious principle that might makes right; patriotism believes on the bedrock truth that right makes might. Nationalism lives to discredit the stern accents of Sinai and the sublime words of the Sermon on the Mount; patriotism dies to make men free, because Christ died to make men holy. Nationalism cries, "There is no god but Caesar"; patriotism urges, "Render unto Caesar the things that are Caesar's, and unto God the things that are God's." Nationalism is the prolific source of class animosities and racial hatreds, selfish interests, political corruption, the spoils system, wars and rumors of wars. Patriotism is the mother of virtue, honor, principle, sacrifice, and boundless good-will.

At the Centennial celebration of American independence, Sidney Lanier wrote the great cantata. In the triumphant passage of its noble climax, the heavenly guide is questioned, "How long, good angel, O, how long shall beloved America endure?" Hear the angel's answer:

"Long as thine Art shall love true love,
  Long as thy Science truth shall know,
Long as thine Eagle harm no dove,
  Long as thy Law by law shall grow,
Long as thy God is God above,
  Thy brother every man below,
So long, dear land of all my love,
  Thy name shall shine, thy fame shall grow." *

Finally, there is no essential connection between religious forms and moral and religious
character. Forms are but the fringe of the robe
of righteousness, and while they may serve as
aids, they prove a poor substitute. Jesus was continually trying to break through the ceremonials
of form which encrusted the heart of Judaism.
And the pitfall of formalism is ever present with
us. George Eliot's description of Hetty in *Adam
Bede* is a typical in stance: "Hetty was one of
those numerous people who have had god-fathers
and god-mothers, learned their catechism, and
gone to church every Sunday, and yet for any
practical result of strength in life, or trust in
death, have never appropriated a single Christian
idea or Christian feeling." Such cases ococur not
only in books. Commissioner McIntyre of the Salvation Army tells of a man who, upon his conver-
sion, was told that he must give himself to some
practical service. "I am unable to do anything,"
he replied, "but I can show you how to fix the gas
meter so it won't register."

Some theologians and preachers have talked

---

* Used by permission of Charles Scribner's Sons.

contemptuously of "mere morality." They might
as well talk of "mere air," "mere sunshine,"
"mere life." As if religion without morality were
not the deadliest of all delusions, the emptiest of
all shams! As if morality were not the very end
and object of all true religion! Mere morality!
Would to God we had more of it, alike among
preachers and people! That is what Christ came
for.

> "He died that we might be forgiven,
> He died to make us good,
> That we might go at last to heaven,
> Saved by His precious blood."

Among the most precious records of Christian
evidence are such passages in the New Testament
as this: "Fornicators, adulterers, thieves, covetous, revelers, extortioners, such were some of
you; but ye were washed, but ye were sanctified,
but ye were justified in the name of our Lord
Jesus Christ."

It is just here that the church stands on a
secure foundation, and "the gates of hell shall not
prevail against it." It is just here that we find
our most priceless treasure, Jesus Christ the
Righteous One. "Get rid of the miracles," said
Rousseau, "and the whole world will fall at the
feet of Jesus." And yet he confessed that this
same Jesus was himself the supreme miracle: "If
the life and death of Socrates are those of a sage,
the life and death of Jesus are those of a God."

"My hope is built on nothing less
    Than Jesus' blood and righteousness:
I dare not trust the sweetest frame,
But wholly lean on Jesus' name;
On Christ, the solid Rock, I stand;
All other ground is sinking sand."

You Can Not Be a Christian Alone

JOSEPH C. SIMONSON

YOU CAN NOT BE A CHRISTIAN ALONE

Let your light so shine before men, that they may see your good works, and glorify your Father which is in heaven. Matthew 5. 16.

IT is wonderful to be a Christian. He is not alone who is a Christian. And solitary loneliness is one of life's heaviest burdens. But the Christian does not bear that burden.

This is true, in the first place, because the Christian has companionship with God. This companionship expresses itself in two relationships: children of God and co-operators with God. And you are not alone when each day you walk with God as His child and His helper!

What does it mean to be a child of God? Well, friend, it is simple but not easy to become a child of God! It is the good tidings of the gospel that we are justified freely by grace when we believe. The gospel says that even in the midst of shame and sorrow over our sin and unworthiness, if we cling to Christ, we still are children of the heavenly Father. Being children of God depends for its certainty upon God, not us. How reassuring that we are children by His love through Christ! If you are a Christian, you are one because of the gift of God. Payment on your part is excluded. God is a King and gives in a royal manner, not expecting anything in return. Kings do not bargain with beggars—they give. And God is a King!

He pours out His mercy where there is faith. But faith is neither payment for nor a condition of God's salvation in Christ. Faith is the blind man crying "Lord, have mercy." Faith is the sin-anguished self-despairing heart crying to God with whom alone there is aid to be found. Faith knows only one possibility — to throw oneself confidently into the vast deeps of God's love. There it experiences the joy of being one of God's children.

And what is the way and power to this experience? It is Christ Jesus our blessed Lord. To repent of one's sin and have faith in Christ the Saviour is so simple that it becomes hard to do. We humans never would have contrived so simple a way of salvation. Human nature instinctively seeks a way out in which we ourselves can do something. We rebel at accepting from God a salvation which is free. Yet His salvation is the only one there is. This is what I had in mind a bit ago when I said that to become a child of God is simple but not easy.

Companionship with God is first a father-and-child relationship. It can be nothing else until it has become at least that. But companionship with God is also co-operation with God. The pastor was in the habit of taking an early morning walk before breakfast. One of his members was an amateur gardener of considerable renown.

This particular morning the pastor walked by this man's home and he was working in his garden. The pastor stopped to talk. "That's a fine garden God and you have made there," said he. "Huh," replied the parishioner, "you should have seen it when God had it to Himself!" Was the man right? I think so. Nature, unaided by man's efforts, is not always and everywhere beautiful. It is a sobering thought for His children that if God's work shall be done in this world, it must be by their hands. If His voice shall be heard, it must be by your speech and mine. If the mind of Christ shall have any place in the world, it can be only by the mind of Christians being like His. God could have decreed otherwise. It is sufficient for me that He asks to have my—and your—active co-operation in bringing His kingdom, hallowing His name and doing His will.

To experience solitary aloneness is to taste futility. Knowingly or unknowingly, all people seek extension of themselves into someone or something outside themselves. We seek inclusion and absorption in that which is bigger, more expansive than we are. And Christians affirm that first such desire is satisfied in a companionship with God through Christ which shows itself in the relationships of being children of and co-operators with God. The traditional prayer of the Breton fishermen still is true: "O God, Thy sea is so great and my boat is so small."

But the Christian is made one not only with God the Father, but in Christ he is made one also

with other Christians. To be in Christ is to have
fellowship with God, but it is also to have fellowship with one another. In that fellowship the
Christian discovers another satisfying alternative
to aloneness. You can not be a Christian alone!
The idea of being a Christian by oneself would
have surprised the apostles. The Lord did not
teach it and it never occurred to the early Christians to think of it even. Christ did speak of His
kingdom—many people gathered under His rule.
In the New Testament Christians are called the
body of Christ, the family of God, the household
of faith, the flock of Christ, the church of God
and the holy city. All these emphasize our faith
as something held in common, in fellowship—not
something which is your and my individual and
private possession.

Not only in early Christian times was there a
recognition of the fact that you could not be a
Christian all by yourself. This year one of our
widely read Christian periodicals is running a
series of articles by the title, "How My Mind Has
Changed in This Decade." It is an interesting
series. Various authors find different things, yet
underneath all the articles so far published lies
a dissatisfaction with the humanistic individualism of these recent years, at least up to 1936.
Though stated differently, what all of them yearn
for is to find social and traditional and historical
confirmation for individual ideas. They are as-
serting that you can not be a Christian alone.
For the last two years the editor of that paper

himself has given voice to the same idea when repeatedly he has said that Christianity's present crying need is for a doctrine of the church. Let one of these writers referred to speak for himself: "The first shift in emphasis [in his thinking] is from a strong tendency toward individualism and contemporaneousness in thought to a recognition of the importance of the Christian tradition. It has been forced upon me that there is an essential irresponsibility about intellectual or religious individualism. To suppose that, . . . thinking or experimenting independently or in the company of a few free-lance writers, I can expect to arrive at significant religious truth, seems to me to represent an absurd overemphasis upon my own insight and upon the wisdom of my generation." (JOHN COLEMAN BENNETT, *Christian Century,* February 8, 1939, p. 179.)

A similar shift of emphasis, he finds, is that now he has a distrust of man and his possibilities to improve himself apart from God. Logically enough, therefore, he also has become skeptical about particular social programs and panaceas. Summing it all up, he writes: "The one idea which seems to run through what I have said more than any other is the idea of the church. It is the carrier of the Christian tradition which molds my thought more than any other system or tradition. It is the Christian movement which makes history and which today mediates Christ to us. The church as an institution is in many places inert and in other places corrupt and apostate, and yet the institution is the framework through which the Christian movement becomes effective." (BENNETT, ibid, p. 181.) The communion of saints, the body of Christ, the fellowship of believers—that is the church! Yea, verily, we were not meant to be Christians by ourselves alone.

It is not difficult to get Americans to accept the values of organization. We are always organizing something. It is so much a part of us that we have been told that if four Americans met in the Sahara Desert the first thing they would do would be to elect a president, vice-president, secretary, and treasurer. Unified, organized action does add a plus something to the efforts of individuals. We recognize this advantage in the church, too. But there is a difference; the church is more than an organization or aggregation of individuals.

American Christianity has an unfortunate tendency. It is to regard the church as some sort of religious club which one may join or unjoin at will. The church is a living thing, not only an organization, but an organism. Its life is organic and therefore like plant life. Now a flower does not join a plant and leave it when it sees fit. Or a baby does not choose a family and resign from it later if displeased with the family. Like this: Paul says we are grafted into the Body of Christ. We may sever our connection, but will die in so doing, though the Body continues to live. It will be shorn of its members, but a man can live without a hand or foot. The hand or foot can not live apart from the man.

Jesus came to minister to us through the instrumentality of a human body. A visible agency was necessary to continue His work of salvation after the resurrection. Such an agency the church is. What His human body was to Christ on earth that the church is to the ascended and exalted Christ. It, too, is His body and Christians are members. The church is the divine society on earth. When we are Christians, we belong to it and no longer abide alone. We have reached up to God and outward to our fellow men. Our souls have lost loneliness, been enlarged and have found destiny in God's ongoing and eternal purposes for us individually and for the world. We will have large horizons; life will be full of zest and high adventure; and we know then that the ultimate end and destiny of man is God's heaven.

Assuredly it is false to the trust committed to us if we do not share such convictions, such joy and peace with all peoples. "Ye are the light of the world," said our Lord. He had a candle in mind as the light, of course. When we bring a candle home from the store we may do one of two things with it. We bought it for the table and to be burned, to be sure. But when we looked at it in the box at home it looked beautiful. We knew burning it would ruin it. So we chose to keep it in the box. That way it would retain its color and shape and would stay beautiful, but would never give any light.

Or we could burn it! Very soon wax might begin to drip and surely the candle would be consumed. It would not long stay a thing of beauty. But—there was light there.

That is the choice we have in life too. We can choose ease. We'll have rest and recreation that way. We'll stay young longer. But there will be no light there. Or we can choose self-sacrificing service for others to the glory of God's name. We can be concerned about our brother's welfare temporarily and spiritually. We will grow prematurely old that way and wrinkles come because we carry the burdens of others. But there is light for Christ then.

In life it is self or God. Either I am the center of my life or God is. The cross is not only a Lenten symbol and reality; it is universal and timeless. Take that willful, proud and arrogant I and draw through it the horizontal bar of God's love and what do you have? The cross! It is the summons unto us to come out of the kingdom of self into the kingdom of God through the grace and power of Christ. The cross is God's compelling call to us to exchange an I-centric heart for a Christ-centric one. In such a change we discover not only God and our fellow men, but we discover our real selves, yet live no longer for ourselves alone. We are on the march to God's heaven with the joyful company of the saints of all time and all places. We are in the church of the living God! Amen.

By Grace Alone

CHARLES LESLIE VENABLE

BY GRACE ALONE

IN 312 A.D., when Constantine was marching against the superior forces of Maxentius who shared with him the divided authority in the Roman Empire following the abdication of Diocletian, he is reputed to have dreamed a dream in which he saw the familiar Christian symbol of the cross with the letters "I. H. S." which he interpreted to mean "In Hoc Signo Vinces" (by this sign conquer). It is not our concern here that Constantine got his signs mixed. The fact is that there is a sign under which Christians are to take their stand and by which we are to conquer and that is the cross of Christ signifying the grace of God.

When Jesus was born in Bethlehem the angels heralded His birth to the shepherds with these words, "This shall be a sign unto you. Ye shall find a babe wrapped in swaddling clothes and lying in a manger." What is the sign of a baby? A baby is a sign of two things: the tenderness at the heart of the universe and the tenderness at the heart of man. A baby has no weapons. It can survive only because of the conquering power of tenderness or grace. What is the sign of the Babe of Bethlehem? It is the sign that God has entered upon the conquest of this earth by grace alone.

When Jesus gave the only reasoned statement
for belief in Him, in the fourteenth chapter of
John, He based it upon three things. The first is
the presumption of God's grace, our right to assume that God is gracious. "Ye believe in God,
believe also in me. In my Father's house are
many mansions: if it were not so, I would have
told you. I go to prepare a place for you. And if
I go and prepare a place for you, I will come
again and receive you unto myself; that where I
am there ye may be also." The second is the perception of God's grace in Him. "He that hath
seen me hath seen the Father." The third is the
possession of God's grace through Him. "Believe
me that I am in the Father, and the Father in
me; or else believe me for the very work's sake.
Verily, verily, I say unto you, He that believeth
on me, the works that I do shall he do also; and
greater works than these shall he do."

In the first chapter of his gospel, John sums up
the whole meaning of Christianity, that is, the
life and work of Jesus, in two verses: "The Word
was made flesh, and dwelt among us (and we
beheld his glory, the glory as of the only begotten
of the Father), full of grace and truth. . . . And
of his fulness have all we received, and grace for
grace." John hinges the whole matter on these
two things: the perception of God's grace in Jesus
and the reception of God's grace from Jesus.

If this is Christianity, then there are three
things which we ought to do about it. In the first
place, we ought to make it our measure. "I say,

through the grace given unto me," writes Paul, "to every man that is among you, not to think of himself more highly than he ought to think; but to think soberly, accordingly as God hath dealt to every man the measure of faith." This is the sin which gets itself mixed up with money, that we think of ourselves as worth a great deal because we have money or not worth much because we have none. Whenever we think soberly, we realize that our worth, to our families, to all those we come into contact with, and to our age is measured in terms of the grace of God which is in us and which sheds itself across other lives. That is our measure and the only one for us to use—grace alone.

In the second place, we should use this as our method. There are four foes which we must meet in life: sin, sorrow, sickness, and suffering, and we must all meet all of them. Religion has the only realism here. Literature, art, education, and science all proceed on the assumption that these are exceptional experiences which may be easily ignored or easily obviated. That is wishful thinking. There is no power of science or wealth which can insulate us against any one of them. Christianity says we must meet them and that we can meet them by grace alone.

We can only look at two of them, sin and suffering. Sin is a terrible thing. It has drenched this earth with blood and filled it with broken hearts and homes from the beginning of time. Have we in religion the power to conquer sin in the earth?

When one is wrong with anyone, he feels mean and acts meanly. When one is right with anyone, he feels happy and acts nobly. Every sin in the world is the end product of a life which in some measure is wrong with God, and every virtue in the world is the end product of a life which is in some measure right with God. The simple fact is that when we see God in His grace like the prodigal's father coming down the road with outstretched arms to receive us back into a right relationship with Him, the conquest of sin has begun in us and in the world. The way to deal with sin is by grace alone.

Suffering, too, is a terrible thing. The total of the world's woe is something no mind can conceive, but Paul gives us an amazing list of what one man can know: imprisonments often, beatings eight different times, once stoned and left for dead, attacks by wild beasts, three shipwrecks, attacked by mobs, waylaid by gangs, hunger and privation, the weariness of long and exhausting journeys and the weariness of long and exhausting labors, and those inner sufferings, the hostility of his enemies, the betrayal of his friends and the dissensions of his churches. Do any of you know any list like this? Yet these were all passing experiences. His sickness was permanent. Of this, he says, "I besought the Lord thrice, that it might depart from me. And he said unto me, My grace is sufficient for thee: for my strength is made perfect in weakness." Remove them? Of course Christianity is the one agency in the world

constantly and consistently working for the removal of these sufferings, but Christianity does
not lure men with the false hopes of that promise.
Christianity functions in present realities. It
equips us to meet the sufferings of life not merely
by the hope of their removal, but also by using
our sufferings as a means of growth in character
and growth in power. With our stripes, others
are healed. Christianity uses that vast body of
inescapable suffering as a means of grace. Christianity, therefore, attacks suffering on both
fronts, and conquers it by grace alone.

The third thing for us to do is to use grace as
our might. The world is locked in a titanic struggle between two theories of power. The one is
the theory of physical force, the other, the grace
of God. The one is the prison theory of life, the
other is the personal theory of life. In a prison
one has everything to make one good and to make
one happy, food, clothing, shelter, warmth, activity, recreation, security, regulation and organization; everything except the free grace of God.
The totalitarian theory of government is not new.
It has been in existence ever since prisons have
been invented. But the results of all the years
have been zero. Prisons do not make men good
and they do not make them happy. Martin Luther
said long ago that the power of government is
only negative. It can chain up the wild beast but
it can not make him tame. That can only be done
by tenderness—by grace alone. Here is something without which men can only first enslave

themselves and then destroy themselves. Our
might for the making of a better world is by
grace alone.

Our church believes in salvation by grace alone.
We believe that it is the only way that the world
can be saved, by God's way as revealed in Jesus
Christ. But our church also believes in something
else. We believe in the means of grace. We not
only believe in the grace of God as our measure,
our method and our might, the channels of God's
power out into the world, but also in the means
of grace as the channels of God's power down into
our lives. As between the two banks of a river
the water flows down to the sea, so through Word
and Sacrament God's grace flows down to you
and me. As the power from the powerhouse
flows over the wire to light this room, so the
grace of God flows through Word and Sacrament
to illumine and transfigure you and me. If that
connection with the powerhouse is severed this
room will be dark, and if that connection with
God is severed, so will we be. We need a clear
track for those cargoes which are to go out into
the world for its redemption and enrichment and
we have it in the grace of God as our measure,
our method, and our might. There are three
clear tracks out into the world. We need a
clear track for these cargoes to come down
into our own lives before we shunt them along
these right-of-ways out into the world and we
have that in the means of grace. Both of these
things, the redemption and enrichment of the

world and the redemption and enrichment of our souls are wrought by grace alone. Let no man block or sever the track at either end.

Religion, as one of my honored teachers used to say, is not a matter of both hands up to God, praying only, "Give me." Religion is not a matter of both hands out to men in helping them. Religion is one hand up to receive power and one hand out to men to transmit it to them. But the power which flows to us and is effective for them is, in both instances, grace alone. "This shall be a sign unto you." God has entered upon the salvation of the world by grace alone.

Choosing the Cross

C. O. BENGTSON

CHOOSING THE CROSS

THE Apostle Paul once made a visit to Athens. While there he met some people who "spent their time in nothing else but either to tell or to hear something new." Paul discussed religion with them and preached to them about the nature of God, about Jesus and the resurrection. He clinched one of his points by quoting from their own poets. It must have been a learned and excellent sermon. We have only a brief outline of it, but that enriches our Bibles much.

But Paul himself seems to have been dissatisfied. From Athens he went directly to Corinth. He has described the state of mind in which he arrived: "When I came to you I came not with excellency of speech. . . . I determined not to know anything among you save Jesus Christ and him crucified. My preaching was not with enticing words of man's wisdom." Thus Paul deliberately chose to narrow down his preaching to one fundamental theme, the cross of Christ.

The choice does not mean that Paul quit being practical. All his writings are filled with practical suggestions. It does not mean that Paul did not know that human nature is complicated and human needs many and varied. His writings are proof in that matter also. It does mean that Paul

41

chose to look upon human life, in its relationship
to God, in the light the cross sheds upon it, that
he intended to find direction for life in the way
that the cross points out. "Enticing words of
man's wisdom" that do not take the cross into
account Paul decided must be put aside as being
without consequence.

Paul's choice of the cross aroused much opposition. That is scarcely surprising. Since Paul's
day Christians have made much of the cross as a
symbol of their religion. They have cast it in
silver and gold, adorned it with precious stones,
and made it a thing of art and beauty. That is
well if the reverse side is not forgotten. Paul's
contemporary opponents saw only the reverse
side. To them the cross was only a horrible instrument of death. Every informed Jew knew
the words of the ancient law: "If a man have
committed a sin worthy of death and he be put
to death and thou hang him on a tree . . . he
that is hanged is accursed of God." Cicero, speaking the sentiments of both Greeks and Romans,
said: "Let the very name of the cross be far
away, not only from the body of a Roman citizen,
but even from his thoughts, his eyes, his ears."
Death on the cross was reserved for slaves and
the vilest of criminals.

Paul was aware that he would arouse opposition. But he had found something in the cross
that was far too good to let go. He put it this
way: "We preach Christ crucified, unto the Jews
a stumbling block, and unto the Greeks foolish-

ness; but unto them which are called, both Jews and Greeks, Christ the power of God, and the wisdom of God." The spirit of the Lord had come upon Paul and to him had been given the grace to see the "deep things of God." In the suffering, death, and resurrection of Jesus the curse changed into a blessing, the ugliness of sin gave way before the beauty of holiness. He jubilated: "Christ has redeemed us from the curse of the law, being made a curse for us: for it is written cursed is everyone that hangeth on a tree."

Outwardly Paul's life was often dificult, but the cross gave harmony and peace to his soul. There was little on this earth to look forward to except trials, persecutions, imprisonments and martyrdom. But he knew an inner abundance of life in his fellowship with Christ. What a glorious confession this is: "I am crucified with Christ; nevertheless I live; yet not I, but Christ liveth in me; and the life which I now live in the flesh I live by the faith of the Son of God, who loved me and gave himself for me." What a beautiful doxology this is: "Thanks be to God who giveth us the victory over sin, over the strength of the law, over death. Thanks be to God who giveth us the victory through our Lord Jesus Christ."

The burden of the doctrine of the cross as Paul preached it runs, then, like this: Man has broken God's holy law and is a sinner. He deserves the curse of which the cross is the horrible symbol and instrument. Man is helpless before this calamity. But Christ has come to man's rescue. In infinite love he has taken the curse upon himself in man's stead. When a man truly believes this and becomes a follower of Christ he is saved from sin, has the peace of God in his heart and lives a blessed life devoted to that which is good. With this doctrine Paul has walked down through the centuries.

We may not have a high regard for the piety of Constantine the Great, but can we fail to be impressed by the circumstance that less than two hundred and fifty years after Paul's death, he found it a good policy to make the cross the standard of his armies and to write thereon the legend: "By this sign conquer?" A far cry, that, from the impassioned words of Cicero.

At the Council of Nicaea in 325, held under the sponsorship of the emperor, Paul's spirit was present. He held the place of honor in the hearts of the councillors. Unmistakably we hear his voice in the grand poem that became the official pronouncement of the council: "I believe in one Lord Jesus Christ. . . . Very God of very God . . . Who for us men and for our salvation came down from heaven . . . and was made man, and was crucified also for us under Pontius Pilate." That has been the confession of the church ever since. It is refreshing and heartening that many present-day leaders of religious thought, who once were dubious, are returning to this foundation.

Luther has written: "Christ has redeemed me a lost and condemned creature, secured and delivered me from all sin, from death and the power of the devil, not with silver and gold but with His holy and precious blood and with His innocent suffering and death; in order that I might be His, live under Him in His kingdom, and serve Him." Those words paraphrase Paul. They were glad words of deliverance to many a tortured conscience in Luther's time. Our children are still memorizing them with profit.

Like Paul, John Bunyan went to jail for conscience' sake. Also like Paul, and from Paul, he learned the secret of the abundant life in the cross of Christ. That was the theme of his matchless allegory, *Pilgrim's Progress*. Christian led astray by Worldly Wiseman, Christian in the Slough of Despond, with the heavy burden upon his back, in the presence of the cross! "So I saw in my dream that just as Christian came up with the cross, his burden loosed from his back, and began to tumble and so continued to do till it came to the mouth of the sepulchre, where it fell in, and I saw it no more. Then was Christian glad and lightsome, and said with a merry heart 'He hath given me rest by his sorrow and life by his death.' " How Pauline it all is! How much we need it today!

"He has given me rest." In this day of hurry and pleasure seeking and worry and heedless sinning, many scarcely know the meaning of that word. The Lenten season invites us to take a bit of time off and sit in quietness at the foot of the cross and behold the sorrow of Jesus on our behalf. By the bitter sorrow of his cross Jesus still sends out the blessed, loving call, "Come unto me, and I will give you rest."

"He has given me life by his death." We need that life. Without it there is nothing but futility and destruction ahead of us. With it there is victory, peace, joy, and fruitful service. With it we can rise above our temptations and failures. With it the awful fear of death is gone. "For me to live is Christ, and to die is gain." Rest, life, this may belong to us all if we choose to take it. "Christ died for all."

Paul's choice of the cross did straiten and circumscribe him, it put him upon a narrow way. That is what the Master said must be, "Strait is the gate and narrow is the way, which leadeth unto life." But it did not imprison His spirit. It gave wings to his spirit. Paul was like the aviator who limits himself to the cramped quarters of his plane and thereby is able to climb into the stratosphere or to encircle the globe. Within the limits of the doctrine of the cross Paul's spirit soared aloft. One day he reached a mountain peak. In our Bibles we call it the eighth chapter of Romans. Paul's heart thrilled with the joy of victory: "I am persuaded that neither death nor life, nor angels, nor principalities, nor powers, nor things present, nor things to come, nor height, nor depth, nor any other creature shall be able to separate us from the love of God, which is in Christ Jesus, our Lord." Oh, for a joy and for a sense of victory like that! We may have it by choosing the cross as Paul did. Amen.

Our Share in Christ's Cross

CLIFFORD A. NELSON

OUR SHARE IN CHRIST'S CROSS

I. WE SHARE ITS GUILT

THERE is only one great theme that is appropriate to us as we come together during these Lenten days to discuss the relation of our lives to God. That theme is concerned with the significance of the cross of Jesus Christ our Lord. If I or any other preacher should miss this emphasis, we would by common consent be counted unfaithful to the great traditions of our church, and it might be said that our speech was irrelevant and indiscreet. It is with sure instincts and mature wisdom that our Lutheran Church urges upon us that we place the accent on Christ's cross these days. Acting like a loving mother and in thorough understanding of our soul's needs, the church draws us aside and whispers quietly to each of us: "If you would be strong for life's tasks, and if you would keep true perspectives in your spiritual vision, take time during this holy season to be still before the man on Calvary. It is in His presence that you will find your own true self. It is there that you will find God. It is there that God will win you for himself and draw you up to high planes of spiritual living." We need, each one of us, this holy interlude in the

It Was for You. 4.

midst of each busy year to renew our devotion
to life's best, and to steady our concentration on
the things that really matter.

In the keeping of Lent there are two traditions
of venerable standing in the Christian community. The one is the custom of making some sacrifice of self-denial in remembrance of what Christ
sacrificed. It urges us to be ready to forego some
luxury or pleasure, and be ready to do some spe-
cial service for God. The other custom is that of
keeping quiet times in meditation at the cross.
Like Jesus, who for forty days and nights went
aside into the wilderness to commune with His
Father and know His purposes for Him, so we
too must take time to be alone with God and listen
to His Word. Both of these traditions are worth
keeping. It is a wholesome thing for us to be
ready to make some personal sacrific; we need
self-control and discipline, and we need it desperately. We ought to be ready to do something
to advance His cause during these days. But first
of all, I hope each of us is determined to be quiet
before Him in contemplation and communion. It
is easier to do things for God than it is to listen to
Him. Sometimes we are so busy running around
doing errands for the Almighty that we have no
time to be still and know that He is God. Our earnest prayer ought to be that we may learn anew
what He has done for us. It is not what we take
out of our lives during Lent that is going to count
ultimately, but what He will put into them. In
His presence we shall look up to find guidance

and direction for better ordering these lives of
ours.

It is sometimes said that the only music truly
native to our American scene are the songs and
melodies that have been beaten out of the hearts
of our once enslaved colored brethren—the negro
spirituals. I am very fond of some of those color-
ful choral outbursts. In all their childlike simplicity, they sometimes reach great depths and
sound the profoundest tones in the human soul.
There is particularly one of those songs that I
never can hear without being deeply moved. The
chorus reads:

"Were you there when they crucified my Lord,
Were you there when they laid him in the tomb?
O, sometimes it causes me to tremble,
Were you there when they crucified my Lord?"

Once I heard Roland Hayes sing those words in
a way that I shall never forget. The melody and
the message have continued to haunt me ever
since. And I do not know that I have ever seen
a large audience of people so thoroughly stirred
and so bound together in a common musical experience. It was as though the lyric voice of that
black man, singing from out of the depth of his
race, and asking that simple question, made the
cross a contemporary reality to us all. It was
deep calling unto deep as our souls caught, even
if only for a moment, the awesome sense of the
way in which we shared in Calvary.

The fact of the matter is that we were there.

On that cruel day when they drove great nails
into the hands and feet of our Lord, something
happened that was not simply an isolated fact of
local history. What took place there is of eternal
significance to every last one of us. The man on
the gallows outside the walls of Jerusalem, in a
profound and mysterious sense which we can not
fully explain, but which we know instinctively
to be true, represented each one of us. And you
and I can go on being glad forever that He represented us so well. There is salvation and redemption for us in the good news that we share
in what He did for us there, and what He was
on Golgotha.

But it is also true that we were not only there,
included in the loving redemptive purpose of
Christ, but that we were there helping in fashion-
ing the events that led up to His cross. When we
ask who it was that crucified Jesus, we open the
story of the Gospels and we answer correctly that
it was the ignorance and evil of a number of people whose names we can mention. It was the base-
ness of a group of high priests and religious leaders whose jealousy and spiritual insensitivity
urged them to the black deed; it was the crowd
that clamored for His death; it was Pilate and
Herod who compromised their souls and allowed
the crime; it was the soldiers that carried out the
act; it was Judas who helped with his base betrayal. Yes, but when we have said all that, we
have not said all. When we examine the reaches
of the whole accumulated sin of crucifixion, we

discover that it is the heaping up of the kind of
sins that lie latent in the human heart. It is the
kind of act against God that is like what our own
sins would make if we had been there. The writer
of Hebrews makes the cross contemporary when
he tells us that those who have known the grace
of the Gospel and then go out into sin again are
those who "crucify afresh unto themselves the
Son of God."

In other words, those who put Jesus to the
cross did the same things that we do when we sin.
The guilt against God is as great for us as it was
for them. We share the great burden of its guilt.
But this is exactly the announcement of the attractive glory of that holy rood. It means so ex-
ceedingly much to us because it was planted at
the gathering place of the sins of the world. It
reaches into the blackness of our hearts and does
something grand and saving to them. The state-
ly words of the creed tell us that He who was
"God of God, Light of Light, Very God of Very
God. . . . for us men and for our salvation came
down from heaven . . . and was made man."
That is wonderful and thrilling. But we go on
and say "was crucified for us under Pontius
Pilate." And still further do the Scriptures go on
to declare that "him who knew no sin he made
to be sin for us." That is the low depth of humiliation to which our Master was willing to go.
To accept the verdict of being made *sin* for us.
We did that to Him. And every time we sin, we
simply take our evil and throw it into the face of

Christ. We recognize the truth in Katherine Pedley's way of putting it:

> "They did not crucify my Lord
> One time alone.
> For I have seen Him on a tree;
> Have watched Him bleed and die for me,
> And, mocking at His agony,
> Have also thrown a stone. . . .
>
> Lord, when we bend the knee before Thy throne,
> How shall we answer, who have slain Thine own?"

Yes, we were there, and we are there with our guilt. Who crucified Jesus? Pilate and Herod did it, yes, that is true. But each time we look around for our own comfort and expediency instead of making way for His truth we too are guilty. The crowd did it, yes, but each time we follow the crowd in its negation of His way of love and go the easy way that everyone goes instead of being transformed and sticking to His will for us, we too are guilty. Judas did it, yes, but each time we are ashamed to confess Christ and refuse to accept the way of suffering love and will do anything for our own advantage at His expense we are becoming like Judas. It is clear to us that we were there.

But all the while He is willing to be sin for us—*"that we might be the righteousness of God."* That was the risk He was willing to make. He believed so much in us because He believed that some of us would be men enough to see that we could not go on doing that, but that, knowing the nobility of His humility, we would be ready for sheer shame to stop our wrong and accept His way. He actually dared to believe that His cross would make us quit our evil and turn us to the right. And it will if we are true to ourselves.

I have in my study a reproduction of a remarkable modern painting done in 1912 by the Frenchman Jean Beraud. He sought to portray the perpetual nature of the Via Dolorosa. The figures pressing with Christ up the hill are not the people of long ago, but they are people out of everyday modern life who are bearing down on His cross and pushing Him along to Calvary. Some brutal men are showing their scorn by blows with clenched fists and shouts of derision. But others, more refined, the man and woman of society in their dress clothes, with jewels and all, are there with their gay laughter. The white-collared organizer of violence is there, even the college professor who is teaching contempt for the way of the cross until a little boy picks up a stone to throw.

It is a tragic picture, this true story of Christ's unending Calvary. Down through the years He has gone toiling on to Calvary. He carries His cross wherever men reject His way. The redeeming side of the artist's conception is a little group of young people off to the side who with the teaching sister have stopped on their way from school to kneel in adoration as He goes on His way.

The way of the cross has never stopped. He was made sin, and He is made sin by us when we turn aside from His way and want our own. But —and this is the important thing—if like children we are willing to humble ourselves in an attitude of learning to take is way of love and sacrifice, then He is able to make of us "the righteousness of God."

"O Saviour of the world, who by thy cross and precious blood hast redeemed us unto God, save us and help us, we humbly beseech thee." Amen.

II. WE SHARE ITS REDEMPTION

God was in Christ reconciling the world unto himself. 2 Cor. 5. 19.

ONE of the earliest vivid recollections I have of my boyhood religious thinking is the memory of my mother in the evening sitting on the edge of the bed reading the history of the Passion to her little boys after they were tucked in. Perhaps the modern child psychologists would not agree with her pedagogy, but during the Lenten season the story of the cross was our daily fare and we boys were so thrilled over the story that we insisted that mother continue, until our eyes had become heavy and we were asleep. I can still remember how my imagination was stirred and how in my childish way I used to think how cruel and treacherous men were to God's Son. If I had been there, how differently I would have acted! How I wished that I had been along as a strong man with a big club to defend my Lord! That cross was all wrong, it ought never to have been. It was the child's way of expressing an instinctive recoil from the cruelty of the cross.

Imagine for a moment that you and I had never before heard the story of the cross. That we were reading it for the first time and reading it in context with the message that it was God's own way of expressing Himself. I think our first reaction would be: Why should there have to be a cross? Why should such a noble and beautiful life have to come to so ignominious and tragic an end? Was there no other way? Was it really necessary that God's love should thus have to find expression? Our conscience cries out and says "No!" Our sympathy is stirred and we say "No!" Our reason with perfect logic also makes answer and says: "'No, this is all wrong!"

And yet the more we consider the place of the cross in the life of the Master and in the structure of our Christian faith, the more we sense how necessary it was. If we should delete out of the records the announcement of the fact of His crucifixion, what we would have left would still be a beautiful chapter in human life, but it would be removing the crowning meaning of all that Christ wanted to bring to us. The story of the cross is the heart of the gospel. It is the cross that has gripped and challenged man to righteousness where the sunnier side of the gospel alone could be of no abiding compulsion. We can not do without it, terrifying as it is, because it is here that God has explained the secret and mystery of life as nowhere else. The theologians down through the years have sought to give us satisfying explanations in their technical language of what the cross means to God and to each of us. But their words of explanation, sometimes cold and hard and unrelated to our own lives, send us back again to the simple Scripture narrative to face Him and to find for ourselves the only thing that can save and redeem us. It is there that we find God doing something creative and redemptive for each of us. Paul caught it up in one great sweeping, cosmic song when he said: "God was in Christ reconciling the world unto himself."

An old medieval painting pictures Christ in His agonies and rather dimly in the background a figure which represents the heavenly Father. He is also on the cross. The nails that are piercing into the frail, sensitive hands and feet of Jesus are going right through into the hands and feet of God. The spear that pierced into the heart of Jesus has cut right through to the heart of the Eternal. Christ's anguish and heartache are the suffering and heartbreak of God. The picture is a crude symbol of the everlasting reality of redemption. The deepest truth we know concerning the cross is that it is the revelation of the wounded and suffering compassion of a loving Heavenly Father. The event of the cross in all its stark and hideous features is for us the opening of a window into eternity where we can see once and for all the kind of love that is aglow at the heart of our universe, in the bosom of our God.

In the last book of the Bible there is something said about the "lamb which was slain from the foundation of the world." There you have it. The cross on Calvary can be dated in human history, but it is timeless and eternal. It covered three terrible hours on a Friday afternoon in the year 30 A.D., but what happened on that green hill far away was but the laying bare of an eternal fact in the being of God. Our God is a suffering God who could not endure to see His children struggling and failing in the carrying of the greatest burden of life—the burden of sin. And so He came Himself to take away the burden and show once and forever that His purpose is a redemptive purpose for our lives.

I have been trying to get at the thinking of some of the philosophers who have been wrestling with the problem of a suffering God. How can He, the Infinite and Eternal One, who is not like ourselves in passions and emotions, be moved so that He can suffer? It is illogical, they say, it goes beyond the categories of human reason. But nevertheless, try as we will to explain it, it is there, inexplicable, and almost absurd, but true. We can not explain the cross, nor the being of God except to say that in the sufferings of Christ it is He who suffered with us and for us to gain victory unto us in all our sufferings and temptations.

When did God first plan the cross? Not when

it seemed impossible that there should be no other
way for His Son to go, but to die. Not even when
the great prophet in the Old Testament stumbled
upon the redemptive principle in life when he
said: "He was wounded for our transgressions
and bruised for our iniquities, the chastisement
of our peace was upon him, and by his stripes we
are healed." No, it goes farther back than that,
back to the very beginning of human life. Back
to the time when God planned that you and I
should have the right to make free choices and
He took the risk of our going wrong if we chose.
Already back there in the garden of creation the
cross was planted in the heart of God. Men could
only be noble and great if they were free to make
their own choice. And God could only be God if
He were ready to redeem and heal the hurts and
wounds that would be inflicted because we would
choose to go our own way. Oh, that we could only
catch the glory of that eternal redemptive purpose! Now and again it is suggested across the
years, as when an Abraham must face the thought
of the sacrifice of his own son, or when a Hosea
senses how only suffering love can win back his
unfaithful lover, or when a Job is reassured that
in all his suffering God is suffering with him. But
it is on Calvary that it all becomes perfectly clear
how this is the very nature of God. It happened
so that no one of us should ever despair again
when we go wrong. For God has suffered with us
and for us to make right what we have spoiled
and misused.

There He is today in the splendor of heaven, and we are told that as He appears before God at the right hand of His majesty, He can be recognized as the Lamb that was slain. He still bears the marks of the cross. All that is only to remind us that the cross is the eternal redemptive fact about God. One day when we come into His nearer presence we shall recognize Him because He still carries the wound prints. Therefore the everlasting song of heaven will always be the song of redemption including thanksgiving and praise and honor and power unto the Lamb, slain from the foundation of the world.

I believe, my friends, that when I say this about Christ, I am saying the most important thing that we can know about God. He came into our world to take upon Himself the consequences of sin that we otherwise would have had to bear ourselves. Like the medieval knight who went into the thick of the battle together with his comrades and when the spears of the enemy were so thick that none could get through, he reached out his arms and drew them all to himself and thus made an open way for his fellows; so in Christ, God took to His own bosom the hurts that otherwise must destroy us and Himself died that we might live and go through the enemy to the other side.

I hope that we shall never forget this central aspect of Christ's cross, because in the remembering and believing of this truth our whole salvation is bound up. The great affirmation is that on the cross God did something for me that I

could not do for myself. He bore the consequences
of my sin. He paid the terrible price, not in silver
and gold, but with His holy and precious blood
and with His innocent suffering and death. We
do not know why it should have cost God so much.
But that is because we do not fully understand
what sin is and what it does to us, and what it
does to God. Only He could deal with the problem of sin. And he did.

Martin Luther, who understood very profound-
ly the deeps of sin and grace in the crucible of
his own experience, once said when he was talking with a man who had a hard time to believe
that sin could cause wrath and grief to God:
"When I see what kind of a man I am, I do not
find it hard to believe in the wrath of God—but
I do find it hard to believe in the grace and love
of God." But the love of the Eternal is real. It is
made certain for us in the cross. That cross is the
meeting place between heaven and earth, and if
we would know God and lay hold on Him it can
be done by laying hold on the cross of Jesus
Christ.

The late Studdert Kennedy has this gripping
bit of verse which he calls "The Sorrow of God":

> "And they say 'E were just the image o' God
>   I wonder if God sheds tears,
>   I wonder if God can be sorrowin' still
>   And 'as been all these years.
>   I wonder if that's what it really means,
>   Not only that 'E once died,
>   Not only that 'E came once to the earth
>   And wept and were crucified?

Not just that 'E suffered once for all
  To save us from our sins,
And then went up to 'Is throne on 'igh
  To wait till 'Is 'eaven begins.
But what if 'E came to the earth to show,
  By the paths o' pain that 'E trod,
The blistering flame of eternal shame
  That burns in the heart of God?
O God, if that's 'ow it really is,
  Why, bless Ye, I understands,
And I feels for You wi' Your thorn-crowned 'ead
  And Your ever-pierced 'ands."

III. WE SHARE ITS FORGIVENESS

And be ye kind one to another, tenderhearted, forgiving each other, even as God also in Christ forgave you.
Ephesians 4. 32.

LAST year, about the time of Lent, a fad
reached its climax among the women of
America. It was the fad of wearing large crosses
ornamented in a hundred different ways as a
piece of jewelry about the neck. I can see no
objection to a Christian wearing a cross or having one in the home as a constant reminder of
Calvary. But I do not see any reason why the
women of the world should want to hang orna-
mental crosses on themselves. It is a sad commentary on our spiritual understanding when the
cross has become simply a fad and an embellish-
ment. But one day our daily papers carried a
large-type advertisement from one of the depart-
ment stores with this line—"Come in and see our

assortment of crosses. We have the latest streamlined crosses." I have been thinking a great deal
about the streamlined cross. And I believe that
we ought to have streamlined crosses. I believe
that we ought to be modern to our fingertips when
it comes to interpreting the meaning of the cross
for our contemporary life and our contemporary
world. For the fact of the matter is that the
cross has always been a modern thing. It is for
every generation to discover for itself where the
implications of Calvary reach into its own life.
It belongs to every one of us to earnestly set about
in the place where we are in making the cross
real in our own experience and our witness among
men.

The cross of Christ has meaning for each one
of us if we are only alert to its challenge. It fits
the needs of our lives as a key fits into a lock and
it opens for us doors into the interior of our souls
and into the heart of God's love that make it possible for us to enter into the spaciousness of life
at its very best. We have spoken about the meaning of the cross in its dimension of redemption,
and we saw how it was the cross of Jesus Christ
that has made the nature of the Eternal plain to
us as the very essence of love and reconciliation.
Now I want to speak about the way in which the
cross spells out a word for the world which is one
of the most important words in our spiritual
vocabulary. It is the word *forgiveness*. And if
we can get at the modern meaning of forgiveness

in Christ's cross, we shall have done ourselves a valuable service.

Think what a history the word "forgiveness" has! The story of the way men labored and sacrificed and suffered and agonized to find cleansing and absolution from their wrongs is the story of the whole romance of the history of religion. Intense prayers, elaborate rituals, bloody sacrifices, temples and altars, scourgings and rugged disciplines, all these and many more are the tools which men have used in their anguished and eager search to know something of the peace and poise of sins forgiven. No wonder that the Psalmist of old wrote a classic poem about the happiness of the man who knows forgiveness.

"Blessed is the man whose transgression is forgiven,
  Whose sin is covered;
  Blessed is the man unto whom the Lord imputeth not
    iniquity."

The history of forgiveness includes the whole upreach of the souls of men, and what is more important it includes the whole downreach of the grace of God. It is to offer the greatest gift that a man can receive that God has put forth His whole saving effort. Like a summary of the entire sweep of God's redeeming grace the prophet Isaiah quotes the word of the Lord as calling for a conference between man and God:

"Come now, let us reason together, saith the Lord;
  Though your sins be as scarlet,
  They shall be as white as snow;
  Though they be red like crimson,
  They shall be as wool."

It Was for You. 5.

In the New Testament, the concensus of all the writers is that the full gift of forgiveness has been offered us as the great fruit of the cross of Christ. "While we were yet sinners," cries Paul, "Christ died for the ungodly. The whole purpose of the cross is revealed in the doing away with sins, sins like yours and mine, and nailing them to the cross, as though the cross were for us the eternal symbol of the fact that they can be done away.

And such it is. We have not caught the supreme significance of Calvary until we have gone straight to the foot of that place where Jesus died and dropped the burden of our sin. I do not know how it can be more simply put than the way Martin Luther once expressed it. He is trying to tell in a few words what it means to be saved. There are only two places, he tells us, where sin can be. Either they are on our own shoulders and we are carrying the burden for ourselves. If that is true, then we are lost. Or else we have placed them on the strong shoulders of the Lamb of God and have let Him lift our burden for us. If we have done that, he says, we are saved.

It is as simple as that and as wonderful. And all down through the years, from the time of the apostles till now, men have been saved, and they have found forgiveness at the cross of Christ. And that is why the cross has never lost its attractive power to people that sin and think about their sins and suffer because of them. And that, I hope, includes us all. Like the pilgrim in

John Bunyan's *Pilgrim's Progress* at the sight of
the cross, we may let our burden roll off our backs
into the open sepulchre. He stood there for a long
time weeping, laughing, and wondering. What a
strange thing that the sight of the cross should
free him from his guilt and his sins! But it does.
It really does. That is the testimony of millions
of sinners who have loved the cross. For those
who believe, the cross of Christ is the highest
symbol of forgiveness.

But mark well: that forgiveness which we
know in Christ is only a part of the full story.
With the forgiveness of our sins there comes a
principle into a believer's life that makes it imperative upon him to go out and show a new spirit
and attitude about forgiving all others who may
wrong or offend him. The teaching of Jesus and
the whole Scripture on that point is perfectly
plain. Once Jesus told a stirring story about a
man who had been forgiven a debt of an enormous sum, so great that he could never repay—
and then when he was asked by the debtor of his
to forgive him a small, insignificant sum, he
refused. Jesus heaped a severe judgment on that
man and went on to say that too often we are like
that. Instead we must be ready, because God has
forgiven us the enormous debt of our sins, to
show a loving and kind forgiveness to every man.
Like the debtor in the parable we are hopelessly
bankrupt before God until He forgives us, and we
must for Christ's sake forgive our brethren any
and every wrong that he might do against us. So

strong and poignant did Jesus make this teaching
of His that He made it perfectly clear that if we
would not forgive our neighbor, then our own forgiveness with God would be null and void. And
to safeguard our remembering this, He taught us
to pray for forgiveness in this way, "Forgive us
our trespasses, as we forgive those that trespass
against us."

Do you get this: the whole ethics of human life
is contained in the word *forgiveness?* You and I
can not be too often reminded of our share in the
forgiveness which we want and seek at Christ's
cross. Because I know people well enough to know
that the best of us go out sometimes and hold
grudges and try to get even with our brother
when he has offended us. When some one injures
us, we keep rubbing it in until it becomes like a
grain of sand in the eye, a swelling infection, instead of removing it and having peace.

We are to forgive just as God forgives. It is
the basic pattern on which Christ planned that
the new kind of life in the kingdom of God was
to be organized. Forgiveness was to be the opening and closing word of every day and of all
attitudes.

There is not space to illustrate the redemptive
power of forgiveness. Only let me remind you
once again of the way in which Jesus lived out
His own teaching on the cross. One day they
nailed Him there. Someone has suggested that
the words of that portion of the Gospel might
have read this way:

"And when they had come to the place which is called the Skull, there they crucified him; and Jesus said: 'Cursed be these men; I will get even with them yet.'"

That would have been the natural and human thing, I suppose. But what did Jesus say? We remember the words: "Father, forgive them, for they know not what they do." That was His way, and that must be our way, too, if we care at all for Him. That was His way of winning the world to God. And there is no other way of winning the world either to God or to ourselves. We who have known His forgiveness must also translate His grace to us into a forgiveness on our part without which we can never know God.

Can you think of anything that this old world of ours needs more today than forgiveness—this world of hatred and suspicion, of force and brute jungle mastery? By forgiving as Christ forgave, we can do as much to save the world in our own place, in our shops and business offices and homes and churches as we can by any other one thing I know.

> "Teach us to love each other, Lord,
>   As we are loved by Thee;
> None who are truly born of God
>   Can live in enmity."

IV. WE SHARE ITS COMPULSION

He laid down his life for us, and we ought to lay down our lives for the brethren. 1 John 3. 16.

SOMEWHERE I once read a poem, the author of which I can not remember, which told the story of a plain man, a factory worker, who lived in a village some distance away from the Atlantic seaboard. He had never had a vacation, and one day his employer told him he might have some days all to himself. He decided to spend them by making his first visit to the seaside. To him who had never before heard the pounding of the heavy waves against the rocks, had never seen the vast expanse of the ocean, it was a thrilling experience. Each day he took his fill of the gorgeous dawns and sunsets and each night he walked along the beach, looking up at the stars and listening to the music of the water. His being there did something to his soul that was akin to a spiritual awakening. Reluctantly at last he had to go back to his own little town and his work-place in the shop. But he was not the same man as when he left. His imagination had been kindled, he had looked on wide horizons and had dreamed of distant shores and the unexplored deep. There were new creative impulses within. New vistas had opened to him. The one phrase I remember from the poem was that the man forever after was plagued by the "torment of the different."

Do you already sense what I am to say to you today about the cross of Jesus Christ? Something

like that is what happens in a man's soul when
he catches even the beginning of a spiritual understanding of the meaning of Calvary. What is
that cross out there in the life of Jesus but a new
and enlarged horizon for our spirits? How it
stirs great aspirations and kindles new hopes and
dreams in men's lives! I pray for each one of us
during these Lenten days that something like that
may happen to us. That as we go gack into our
ordinary, commonplace round of duties it shall be
with a new music running through our lives, and
the tugging of heavenly desires drawing us up to
the highest planes of noble living. I think all of
us would need to have the "torment of the different" from a redeeming experience of the cross
to stab our spirits awake, and make us sensitive
to the hidden things of Christ's kingdom.

I am sometimes afraid we are so sure we know,
because of constant repetition, all the facts of
religion, that we are never looking for the glad
surprises and the ever-deepening insights that we
must share in order to grow spiritually. And so
we go on doing the same old things and never
lifting ourselves beyond the humdrum, never leaving the beaten path that we have been always
walking. In a letter of the late T. E. Lawrence,
better known as Lawrence of Arabia, recently
published, he writes this characteristic of the
Arabs: "They go through life without turning
any corners or climbing any hills." Too many of
us are like that. We avoid the call of the Spirit
that asks us to keep turning into better avenues

of service and we are so afraid to do any spiritual climbing.

But the cross asks us to start climbing up the hill of Calvary with Christ. It is almost startling to have John tell us in the text chosen that the cross of Jesus is not only a place of our redemption, but is an example for us, that we must also be willing to lay down our lives for the brethren. In other words, we must also take up our cross and like Christ give ourselves in redemptive service.

Let us be very reverent before this thought. Martin Luther says in one passage that each of us is to be, as it were, a Christ to our fellow man. Each of us is called to carry out a redemptive task through our lives. Do you remember that when the disciples were gathered in the upper room, the Master said to them: "As my Father hath sent me, so send I you." Think of it. We are called to the same task as Jesus. He says so Himself.

Do not misunderstand me. There is, of course, a vast gulf fixed between us and our Saviour. No one of us can so live or die that men shall find their eternal salvation through us, but there is a real sense in which each one of us is called to be the carrier of the redemptive life of Christ, so that men shall have through us the power of Christ made manifest. We are called to go through life healing and encouraging, helping and cheering, and putting His redemptive power to work. Thus it was that He planned that there should be brought new life to this old world.

The New Testament speaks of the church as the body of Christ and each of us as members, sharing fellowship with Him and taking from Him redemptive strength to bind up the wounds of the world. We must not forget our dignity in being called to have a share in doing the work that He did upon earth. What Jesus was for a moment of history these 1900 years ago, He has called His church to be for all time and we as limbs and members of it are to make sure that we are doing a redemptive task in the area where we are placed.

This is the active and busy side of our religion which we must not forget or neglect. Sometimes I think of religion as being very much like the business of falling in love. There is the romantic side of falling in love, the thing that the poets are forever talking about. But that is only one part. The time comes when two young people are so much in love that they want each other forever. Then it is not all song and romance and cooing words; it means that they will both be busy doing things to create and keep alive a home. There is work to be done, and some of it difficult and exacting. Just so in religion. There is the mystic sense of fellowship, and worship, and the romance of knowing God which is basic and important and true. But religion is more than that. It is more than singing hymns and warming our hearts emotionally at the fires of prayer and faith and

friendship with God. This we must never neglect
to the hurt of our souls. But beyond that God
asks, and Christ on His cross expects, that each
of us shall go out in the world and give our share
in redemptive service. And even when there is
little romance in our service, we must remember
that there was little romance in the hard days of
Jesus and the rouogh, bleeding trudge up the hill
to Calvary. There was little romance in the ach-
ing pain and torture of those fierce hours on the
cross. But this was His purpose and He went to
that cross with steadfast determination.

Was there joy for Christ in going to the cross?
Yes, for we are told that "for the joy that
was before him he endured the cross, despising
shame." But it was not all joy. There was pain,
too. Is there joy for us in carrying Christ's
cross? Yes, most assuredly. But it is joy and
pain. Never the one alone, but always the two
together.

I do not know many of you personally to whom
I am speaking. I can not say to you exactly what
your cross is or must be; but I do know that if
you want to follow Him you must be willing to
grasp some cross where you can give yourself in
redemptive service in the spirit of Jesus Christ.
Perhaps it is first of all in your home where you
must start anew now and live redemptively. Perhaps the area in which you have your daily work
is desperately needing the principles for which
Jesus stood to be applied. I do not know of many
businesses that do not need it and need it des-

perately. Perhaps there are places of service in your church which are needing a redemptive task. I know that most of the churches which I am acquainted with, my own included, are needing people who will do work for the Master in the spirit of Christ.

This world is groaning and travailing for the revelation of the sons of God. Are you going to be willing to do your share to witness and work for Him?

Mr. E. C. Montague, the English novelist, has a very fascinating story which he calls "Rough Justice." In it he tells the story of little Bron who was brought for the first time to the church where his uncle was the vicar. In church he watched the service, the singing of hymns and the saying of prayers. Then his uncle mounted the pulpit and preached his sermon. It was the story of the best man that had ever lived. Bron listened intently. The man had done nothing but good, but at last they took him out and did him to death on a cruel cross. His uncle went on to say that the Man was not dead, but lived again and now He was looking for people who would go out and do for the world as He had done. Bron was thoroughly moved, and he could not understand why people were so calm about that great announcement. They sang a hymn and went out as though nothing strange had been said. Bron instead sat in his pew and sobbed. Finally his nurse said to him, "Bron, you mustn't take it so much to heart, people might think you were queer."

There was one who took it so much to heart
that he went to death because of the world outside. Are we ready to take to heart His message
and the compelling challenge of His cross?

V. WE SHARE ITS GIFT OF LIFE

*For God so loved the world, that he gave his only be-
gotten Son, that whosoever believeth on him should not
perish, but have eternal life.* John 3. 16.

HAVE you ever stopped to think what a mysterious thing it is just to be alive? To be a
part of this throbbnig, pulsating, vital universe
is a puzzling and mystifying thing. Sometimes
it is a good thing for us to get away from the
world of man-made gadgets and buildings and
dynamos and human creations, and feel ourselves
just a part of God's created world, sharing the
gift of life with all living things. We used to
divide the world into animate and inanimate objects, but today the physicist tells us that every
part of our universe is alive with atomic energy.
The creation of life is a magnificent thing. We
think we can see life, we can talk about it, we can
try to define it, we can use it, but what it is in its
essence and ultimate reality is veiled from our
eyes. All we can do is reverently to thank God for
it and let it testify to the vastness in the reaches
of the infinite power of the Eternal. Michelangelo
has tried to picture the moment of the creation
of man on the ceiling of the Sistine Chapel in

Rome. It is the moment when God touches man with His finger and he becomes a living soul.

But I am thinking today of that still higher gift of life which God gives when the Holy Spirit touches a man's spirit with His marvelous creative power and there is given a higher and nobler kind of life. That is the kind of life that John is speaking of in the familiar words of our lesson for today. Throughout the New Testament it is made clear to us that God entrusted to Christ the quality of life which is known as eternal, and through Him has offered that sharing of His own life to us. It is the kind of life which we have from God when we are born again into His world. Mysterious, and unseen, but it is the real life of God given to us through faith in Jesus Christ. That is the kind of life we must covet and nourish within if we would really be alert and aware.

For what is life? Is it simply to exist; to eat, to sleep, to go about our daily round of duties and fulfill the impulses of our natural selves? If that is all there is for us, then we are on the same level as the beast and we reach none of the higher levels of which our souls are capable.

Or is it to find our place in the world of men and make the most of it for ourselves; getting and spending; grabbing and acquiring; pushing and jostling one another in the mad race for laying hold on as many things as possible; and then going out like a snuffed candle? Again, if that is all we have, then it is a real question whether there is any meaning to it, and if it is worth the

effort after all. Then Voltaire's comment on life
is true: "The end of it is dreary, the middle
worthless, the commencement ridiculous." It is
tragic to see so many people make nothing more
of it than that.

But what is life? Listen to the definition that
Jesus gave of it. "This is life eternal, that they
should know Thee the only true God, and him
whom thou didst send, even Jesus Christ." That
is real life, if we believe at all in spiritual values.
Only from a true relation with God can we find
life abundant, true, and satisfying.

E. P. Oppenheim has put it in a poem which he
calls "Night." He pictures a conversation between
a scientist, a poet, and a priest. Each of them has
spoken and now the priest is putting in his word:

"Man of song and man of science,
  Truly you are as people on the outside of a house
The one of you sees only that it is made of stone, and its
          windows of glass, and that fire burns on the hearth;
And the other sees that the house is beautiful and very
          human.
But I have gone inside the house
And I have lived with the host in the house,
And I have broken bread with him and drunk his wine
And seen the transformation that love and awe make in
          his brain;
For that house is the world and the Lord is my host and
          my Father.
It is my Father's house.

Enough? I see what is enough.
Machinery is enough for the scientist,
And Beauty is enough for the poet;

But in the hearts of men and women, and in the thirsty
    hearts of little children
There is a hunger, and there is an unappeasable longing
For a Father, and the love of a Father.
For the root of the soul is mystery,
And the Night is mystery;
And in that mystery men and women open inward unto
    Eternity
And know love, the Lord,
Blessed by His works, and His angels, and His sons
    crowned with His glory."

This is the dignity and nobility of life; to know
God and to share the gift of His own life. That
was the gift that God wanted us to have through
Christ and His cross. There is not enough of possessions or things on the face of the whole earth
to satisfy one hungry soul, who is reaching out
for the fullness of that for which his interior soul
is asking. We have not discovered the true meaning of the cross of Jesus until we are ready to go
up to Him and ask that we may have a share in
His gift of life, that we may have within us the
same kind of being which He had so richly and
which was His to give to men. "In him was life;
and the life was the light of men."

And this is His gift through the holy miracle
of His broken body which has become food for
our souls. In the upper room Jesus gave to His
men the wine and the bread and said: "This is my
body, given for you" and "This is my blood, shed
for you." It is sacramental language and it contains a mystery beyond our fathoming, but the
essence of it is that through Christ there is a

stream of life flowing which is meant for all who believe on Him. It is the giving to us of God's new life to transform and make us like Himself. Never can we know perfectly here what it is to share the full life of God. We are too humanly delimited by our sins and our very human nature. But there is this gift for us through faith in Christ.

Don't you see what it means? Christ was, as Paul says, the second Adam. He came to found a new race of men to make a new world. The old natural man was not good enough for His kingdom. Only making men over again in His likeness would be good enough. And this, I take to be the meaning of the power of life that we are to receive through His blood. In actually sharing His person, His body, and His blood, we become partakers of His real presence. Such language becomes real and tangible for us at the altar of Holy Communion, but it is meant to be a sharing of His real presence in service and redemptive life through us in our daily witness in the world of men.

The kernel of what I am saying is this: if we would share the cross and all it means for us, it is not enough that we go to the cross simply to adore and to admire Him. Christ is not looking for admirers, but (again in sacramental language) He is looking for people who will take Him and assimilate Him and share His very life with the world.

May I ask of you then that, by the mercies of

God you present your bodies a living sacrifice and go to Him and kneel lowly before Him and ask for His life within?

In Copenhagen, in the Church of Our Lady, is the well-known statue by Thorwaldsen of the Christ with outstretched arms saying: "Come unto me." I was told when I went to see it that the only way to really see that statue is to go to the altar rail and kneel down and look up into the wonderful features that the artist in a moment of inspiration created. I did so, and I had a spiritual experience. That is the only way in which any of us can know Christ; by bowing lowly before Him, looking up and asking for His love, His mind, and a share in His life which can through us be given to the world.

Yes, we have a share in Christ's cross. During Lent let us allow the cross of Calvary to become so real to us that it actually becomes imprinted on our hearts and engraved on all of our life's witness. I want to make Savanarola's Lenten prayer my own as I go through the holy days of this season:

> "Jesus, may our hearts be burning
>   With more fervent love for Thee;
> May our eyes be ever turning
>   To Thy cross of agony;
> Till in glory parted never
>   From the blessed Saviour's side,
> Graven on our hearts forever,
>   Dwell the cross, the Crucified."

Amen.

It Was for You

OTTO MEES

IT WAS FOR YOU

I. THE VICARIOUS CHRIST

Christ also suffered for us, leaving us an example, that ye should follow his steps: Who did no sin, neither was guile found in his mouth: Who, when he was reviled, reviled not again; when he suffered, he threatened not; but committed himself to him that judgeth righteously: Who his own self bare our sins in his own body on the tree, that we, being dead to sins, should live unto righteousness: by whose stripes ye were healed. 1 Peter 2. 21–24.

"THAT we should follow his steps." What a challenge! Does it thrill you to be invited to join Him on His journey? Are you, who bear His name, anxious, eager, and proud to be in His company? Have you, as a Christian, ever hesitated or even flinched in your loyalty and devotion when it became apparent that to follow the way the Master went might threaten your ease, your comfort, or your safety? There, on the dusty highway, we see Him walking, His face steadfastly set to go to Jerusalem—cheerfully, courageously, determined.

To follow the Christ into Jerusalem, and all the way up Calvary's hill, to mourn at the tomb in Joseph's garden—that requires faith and humility. Human pride rebels against it; desire for physical security discourages it; hope of material advantage forbids it. To the sharp and pointed question: *Why* this tremendous, dramatic tragedy which brought an innocent victim to an ignominious death? there is only one answer:

IT WAS FOR YOU

It was just twelve years ago that a burning wish of many years had its fulfillment for me. I stood on the streets of Jerusalem, the city and the scene of my Saviour's passion. From that moment on the Bible became a new book to me. History was re-enacted in swift panorama before my mind's eye. Things and events which I had learned in early youth and which form the background for every Christian's thought during the Lenten season became both beautifully and terribly real. Jerusalem, as someone has written, "is like a stringed instrument, every touch upon which brings forth some sweet or discordant sound, for it vibrates at every turn with some suggestion or passage of the Word of God."

We desired, as nearly as possible, to follow the way the Master went. A native of the city was our guide. It was very early. Our course took us out into the village of Bethany, where Simon the leper lived. It is interesting to note that the Saviour's passion began in a home. Here He received the loving ministration of a plain but devoted woman. The most precious gift she had was not too good to be given in His service and His cause. And that humble service was destined to be talked

about, to be held up as an example worthy of
emulation, in all the world, throughout the ages.
I wonder why?

A comparatively short walk brought us to the
crest of a hill known as the Mount of Olives.
Nestled in a pocket formed by surrounding hills
lay the city with its minarets and towers. The
road seemed to be teeming with people. The
crowd was almost blocking the progress of a man
riding on a beast of burden. They were excited.
They were spreading their cloaks on the ground
for Him to pass over on them—a sign of willing subjection, as to a royal personage. Palm
branches lay strewn before Him. It was a glorious
reception, a march of triumph, a conquering hero
acclaimed by His happy people. Hosannas filled
the air! "Blessed is he who comes in the Lord's
name" is the mighty chorus! Then silence. The
scene changes. We are in the city streets. Again
a crowd is milling about. Again they seem excited. Again they are shouting with high-pitched
voices. But now it is not a song of joy, no theme
of praise. It is anger and passion that we hear.
"Away with him; let him be crucified; we have
no king but Caesar." The same man, the same
people! How fickle are men — today accepted,
tomorrow rejected; today praised, tomorrow
blamed; today blessed, tomorrow cursed. *I wonder why?*

Some time later we found ourselves in a room
on the second floor of a modest building. A table
seemed to be spread before us. Around it sat

Jesus with His twelve most intimate followers. They were observing an annual custom, a holy fast day. We might well call it the first Brotherhood meeting. The conversation was serious and instructive. Questions were asked and answered by the leader. He spoke to them earnestly and they listened intently. When the time for adjournment came they joined in singing a hymn which helped to unify them in mind and purpose. As they went out together, one of their number was not among them. Earlier in the evening he had slipped out—alone—to carry out the crime of the ages—under the cover of a dark night to betray his Master. *Why did this have to be?*

When evening came, our little group of six found and followed the narrow way that led to Gethsemane, over the ravine through which flowed the brook Kidron. We wanted to be alone. It was very dark. A drizzling rain was falling. We recalled the conversation between Jesus and His disciples on that fateful occasion two thousand years ago: "All ye shall be offended because of me this night." Soon we were among old olive trees. The quiet of death was around us. Then there seemed to arise from the not distant shadows a voice in agonizing prayer: "Father, if it be possible, remove this cup from me: nevertheless, not my will, but thine be done." But He had to drink it. Do you know why? Now came the sound of tramping men, nearer and nearer. Lighted torches appeared, the clank of swords and staves was heard as though to mortal

combat—a familiar greeting: Hail, Master!—
an affectionate kiss—a gentle recognition: My
Friend—and the foul deed was done. Why? To
climax the tragedy, those who alone might offer
comfort and support in His trouble forsook Him
and fled. He had to tread the wine press alone.

We came back to our hotel—tired, cold, de-
pressed. A large group of American tourists
were gathered in the dining room. They, too, had
spent the day visiting places and scenes familiar
and sacred to all Christians. They, too, had followed the Christ to Jerusalem. They were a merry
crowd. Joking and loud laughter filled the hall.
Presently one of their number arose and cried in
a loud, scoffing voice: "We have seen so many
holy places today; everything around here seems
to be holy. Does anyone want to pray?"

As we recede by centuries from the time and
scene, we are prone to lose sight of the *personal
significance* of that which happened to our ac-
knowledged Master. Do you ever ask yourself
the frank but fair questions: What has all this to
to with *me?* Is it my fault? Am I to blame? You
must find an answer. Or—you must acknowledge
that you do not know *why* Christ had to suffer
and to die. Go with Him to Jerusalem and follow
His weary and painful course. The petals of the
Rose of Sharon are dropping off, one by one, as it
is being crushed. Ruthlessly stripped of color
and fragrance, it "hath no form nor comeliness."
"There is no beauty that we should desire Him";
"He was despised and rejected of men." But it

will also be brought home to you with inescapable
clearness that He was bearing *our* griefs, that He
was bruised for *our* iniquities, that the Lord has
laid on Him the iniquity of *us all,* that with His
stripes we are healed. To be reminded of this
may be humiliating, but it is also comforting. It
may be distasteful, but it is truth, terrific truth,
which can not be explained away. Listen! Listen
intently as the story is once more unfolded to you.
You will hear, stealing out of the night shadows
of Gethsemane's garden the sound of a traitor's
kiss. Your indignation is aroused at such base
betrayal. But are you forgetting: *It was for you?*
You will hear the quiet and dignified defense of
one who is being falsely accused. Your sympathy
goes out to Him who seems helpless in the face
of testimony by hired witnesses. *It was for you!*
You will hear the resounding slap of a hostile
hand on a pale cheek. Your anger kindles at the
insult. *It was for you!* You will hear the "sisch"
of a tearing garment in mock piety, by a High
Priest, as he elicits from the crowd the verdict:
"He is guilty of death." You turn pale at the injustice. *It was for you!* You will hear the crack
of the scourge as it sinks deep into the flesh of
the quivering victim. The very thought is sicken-
ing. *It was for you!* And underneath the voices
and the noises perhaps you can detect the sound
of tired feet, dragging their weary way over the
city streets, up Calvary's hill, under a crushing
load. Your heart melts with pity. *It was for you!*
Then—the hollow sound of a hammer driving

nails through soft flesh. You shudder! But—*it was for you!* Finally the terribly triumphant cry, piercing the mysterious darkness: It is finished! The atoning work is done. And you can hear the hills surrounding the city echoing and re-echoing one to another the wonderful assurance: *It was for you!*

Come then, and let us follow Jesus as He sets His face steadfastly toward Jerusalem—here, during the coming weeks, and in our several churches.

Upon this foundation rests the Christian Church. Christian faith embraces a Saviour. He did for me what I could not do for myself. This is the Christian's Christ.

II. The Defiance

When Pilate saw that he could prevail nothing, but that rather a tumult was made, he took water, and washed his hands before the multitude, saying, I am innocent of the blood of this just person, see ye to it. Then answered all the people and said, His blood be on us and our children. Matthew 27. 24–25.

YESTERDAY we followed the hard and bitter course of Jesus from the pleasant home in Bethany, over Olivet's brow, to His triumphant entry into the city. We traced His experience with His disciples as they sat together like brothers; how they sang a hymn together and went out into the dark night, over the brook, into the garden of Gethsemane. We heard Him pray, "Father, if it be possible, take this cup from me." But it was not possible. He knew it—His work had to be finished, and He steadfastly set His face to meet His doom. It was for *me* and for *you,* that we might have hope.

This noon we are standing near a row of three crosses. We are on the execution grounds. Criminals, malefactors, are brought out here to pay the price of their evil deeds. Yes, it is almost too gruesome to describe—but it is true, terribly true —blood is flowing freely from wounds in hands and feet and from wounds in the body. The people pass by and make their sneering remarks about the unfortunate victims. But let us stop a moment! "See yon mother bowed in anguish, who beside the cross doth languish." Her son was dying and she could not help it. Her child was cursed and she could not remove the stain. It was the curse of sin. What crime did He commit? Was it *His* sin? It was for *me* and for *you.*

A few hours before, a sharp argument had taken place between Pilate, the governor, and the people, goaded and coached by the priests. Fain would he have released Jesus. He felt that an injustice was being done. He understood the sinister motives of the envious priests. He reasoned and fenced with them, but he had to admit defeat. The tragedy could not be prevented.

Out on the Via Dolorosa He staggers under the weight of the cross. Along the way there were women—with children—they wept for pity. Jesus turns to them and with even voice admonishes,

"Weep not for me, but for yourselves and your children."

What may have prompted this warning? The echo of the wild, defiant cry still resounded through the city streets: "His blood be upon us and on our children." Think of it—they invited it as a *curse!* Have you ever stopped to consider what it means to be guilty of blood? Guilty—this word alone should make us wince. It involves that we are justly chargeable with a crime. And guilty of *blood,* of causing undeserved death, the worst of all crimes—isn't it shocking? Can you picture to yourself Cain of old, a fugitive and vagabond, a marked man, restless and haunted, because he was guilty of shedding his brother's blood? Visualize, if you will, a king, sitting in splendor on a throne, vested with unlimited power and authority—but cringing before the accusing finger of Nathan the prophet who bared his guilt with the words: "Thou art the man!" How Pilate dreaded the very thought! We can almost see him grow pale as he protested: "I am not guilty of His blood. If He dies, it is not my fault. The case is yours, see ye to it." But the people, swayed by uncontrolled passion, wildly accept the challenge. They are not afraid. They gladly assume all responsibility. "We have nothing to fear. His blood be upon us, and upon our children." Is this spirit of self-assurance perhaps the forerunner of a more modern defiance to divine authority and responsibility found in the arrogant contention:

"I am the Master of my fate,
I am the Captain of my soul,"

—the *lie* of the ages.

But what has all this to do with me, and with you? Were you there when they crucified my Lord? Yes, my friends, you were there. You can not dissociate yourself from the scene and its sad outcome. The question still persists, Why all this? The answer is, Sin. Do you ask, Whose sin?

The wages of sin is death. This is a hard saying; it is almost repulsive to the modern mind, but it is still true. That, and that alone, made Calvary's cross necessary. I know that the reality of sin is being questioned. Modern philosophy likes to speak of a new conception of sin. It is a favorite deception to attempt to explain out of existence that which is unpleasant and undesirable. There is a tendency to modify and to soften the exceeding sinfulness of sin. But it is a poor service to try to dispel fear by belittling or minimizing the real danger.

And the penalty of sin? "Well, perhaps we must pay in our bodies for our mistakes and faults here on earth. That the soul shall be lost —separated from God eternally because of what some call Sin—that can not be! That doctrine is inherited from the Middle Ages. It is not in harmony with God's great love toward men." But sin is first and foremost an offense against God. It is a transgression of God's law. Whether you like it or not, the same God has declared, "The

soul that sinneth, it shall die." Has anyone, or
any group, the authority to commute this sen-
tence? If so, who? Or are we hearing today a
revised echo of what was cunningly suggested to
our ancestors in Eden's garden: "Should God
have said that? Surely not. That must be a mistake. Ye will not die." As we stand at the foot
of Calvary's hill, let us rather heed the words of
the hymn:

> "Ye who think of sin but lightly,
>   Nor suppose its evil great,
> Here may view its evil rightly;
>   Here its guilt may estimate."

And what about the children? Not content to
invite a curse upon themselves, they defiantly load
the guilt upon their children. It is also a law of
God that the sins of the fathers are visited on the
children. And this is a statement which should
be burned into the consciences of every one of us.
It is a fearful truth. Have you ever visited an institution for the care of feeble-minded children
and young people? Investigation will reveal that
a shockingly large percentage of the inmates are
the innocent victims of the sins of their parents.
Every child has a right to be well born. Too many
are deprived of this privilege because thoughtless
persons have failed to weigh the far-reaching
consequences of their sin. Children have a right
to expect from their parents a heritage of which
they at least need not be ashamed, and which will
not serve as a ball and chain around their future
life. What parents will deny their responsibility

for the physical well-being of their offspring?
Is it any less a sacred duty to direct and guide
their spiritual development? How shall they believe in Him of whow they have not heard? From
whom shall children learn to know Jesus as their
Saviour rather than from the lips and lives of
their parents? The soul's life and blood of children whose parents have taken lightly or have
ignored the injunction: "Ye fathers, bring up
your children in the nurture and admonition of
the Lord," will be demanded of *them*. How important is it to you fathers and mothers to know
that your children are receiving spiritual nourish-
ment? Or don't you care whether their hungry
souls are fed? Is it none of your business? Would
you rather that they grow up without having
learned to know and to believe in Christ? Are
you ready to join the crowd which defiantly
cried: "His blood be upon our children. We will
take the chance."

The comfort of a Christian faith lies in the assurance of the forgiveness of sins. The message
of Christianity to the world is, that there is a
redemption. But the same source advises us:
"Without shedding of blood there is no forgiveness." And redemption can not be purchased except the price be paid. "For ye are bought with
a price." The Apostle Paul most emphatically tells
us that Christ purchased His church with His
own blood. Without that conviction, what can the
Lenten season mean for you? In Christ we have

redemption through His blood, the forgiveness of
sin. This, too, is essential for Christian faith.

III. Calvary's Answer

*Then answered all the people and said: His blood be
upon us and on our children.* Matthew 27. 25.

YESTERDAY our meditation brought us the
record of a most unusual contrast. On the one
hand an unbelieving Roman governor, who yet
had a sense of justice, pleading for the life and
freedom of an innocent prisoner; on the other
hand a wild mob, led and goaded on by priests
and high priest, the religious leaders of the people, demanding His execution. "I find no fault in
Him! What evil hath He done?" is the argument on the one side. But the defiant echo was:
"Away with Him! Crucify Him! His blood be
upon us!" In their blind frenzy, without weigh-
ing the cost, they were willing to assume full responsibility for His death. They even invited upon
themselves a *curse*. But let us not be too quick
in expressing horror or in passing judgment. If
you or I would have been there among them, I
wonder on which side we would have found ourselves! Are you sure of the answer?

A few days before the tragic scene we have just
pictured, we find Jesus together with His few
faithful disciples walking one morning from
Bethany, where He had spent the night with
friends, toward the big city. He was hungry.

Along the road stood a fig tree, resplendent in
healthy looking leaves, which gave promise of fine
fruit. He approached it to pick some figs, to satisfy his hunger. But when he found that the tree
was barren of fruit he *cursed* it. The next morning as they came along the same way, the disciples saw that the tree was dead, dried up from
the very roots. Peter remembered about it and
said: "Look, Master! The fig tree that you cursed
is withered up." And the only answer he received
was: "Have faith in God." Is it a light thing to
be under the divine curse? If not, what can be
done to escape it, or not to deserve it? Jesus had
a right to expect abundant fruit, but found nothing but leaves. He also had a right to expect faith
and greater loyalty on the part of those among
whom He had lived and wrought. Had He not
taught them daily; had He not preached to them
wherever occasion offered—in the temple, in their
synagogues, in their homes, in the fields, along
the seashore, until their hearts were warmed and
they followed Him in multitudes? Had He not
healed their sick, relieved their sufferings, given
sight to the blind and hearing to the deaf—even
life to their dead—until they sang His praises and
worshiped Him? But when the test came, when
He hungered to have them near Him, when He
needed their support and encouragement to finish
the task for which He came—which was to seek
and to save those who are lost—He found no
fruit—nothing but leaves! Here again the Scripture was fulfilled: "He came unto *His own* and

His own received Him not." Oh, the heartache of being *rejected, repudiated, forsaken* by His own people! Betrayed, not by *outsiders,* but by His own household.

But will the Christ be less disappointed when He comes to you and to me looking for fruit? He has a right to expect it. Has not the preaching of the gospel resounded in our midst without let or hindrance? Has He not moved among us continuously with His means of grace, calling to repentance and faith? Do we not have the glorious Easter message of an empty tomb, a living Lord? Is it not reasonable that we should be like trees, planted by the rivers of water, which bring forth their fruit in their season? What will the Master find? Nothing but leaves, which would invite his curse?

And what will He find in our children! Shall they, too, be subject to God's curse because of our neglect? Would you do such a thing? Leave your children the heritage of sin, and then leave your children without a remedy or cure for that sin?

But God is better to us and ours than *we* are! In His beneficent plan the curse which the people invited upon themselves and on their children become a *benediction.* Through the tumult of the throng, the wild cry for a victim which filled the air and prevailed over every well-meant effort to restrain them and to be fair, there comes another voice—a still, soft voice, perhaps only a whisper. It is pleading, it is laden with pity, sweetened by love, warmed by an all-embracing *mercy.* No, the mob does not hear it, but it pierces the heavens and reaches the very highest tribunal—the throne of God: "Father, Father, forgive them, for they know not what they do." Is that true? Did they not know what they were doing? Could or should they not have known? He had testified under oath: "I am the Christ," the Messiah who was promised by the prophets. No one could successfully dispute His claim. History, the records and His personal life were all in His favor. The civil court, after a severe and searching trial, pronounces Him a just man. The judge had challenged His accusers to show what evil He had done. They could not prove a single charge. They had heard the highest authority in the land say: "I find no fault in him." "Yet, in the face of all that *knowledge* they defied God and cried: His blood be upon us and on our children." But in Calvary divine justice is overshadowed by the divine mercy. There is no vindictiveness here, no eye for an eye, or tooth for a tooth, no meting out according to just desert. This heartless rejection, this heartbreaking experience he accepted and bore because it meant that in the end we might become His own and live under Him in His kingdom. Again, there flashes out of the darkness of the shadaw of His death the blazing device: "It was for you" which for many is so hard to understand. He died that we, yes, those who brought Him to His death, might be forgiven. He paid the penalty of a guilty one, that we who have the guilt and deserved the fate which befell Him might be *free*. That, and that alone, made it possible for the Apostle Paul to say: "There is now no condemnation to them which are in Christ Jesus." What a tremendous statement that is! His blood *is* upon us and on our children. Yes, there came out of his cleft side—blood; it moistened the earth. But from the ground that blossomed red there came also life, new life, *life* that shall ever be. The curse, which foolish, blinded man invoked upon himself, love—incomprehensible love, has turned into the choicest blessing. The defiant cry was: His blood be upon us and on our children. The reassuring answer comes to us from the very court of heaven: "Ye are justified by His blood!" The insistent clamor was: His blood be upon us and on our children. The comforting answer applies to you and to me: In Him we *have* redemption through His blood. The hills of Judea still reverberate with the loud challenge: "His blood be upon us and on our children." But from Zion's holy hill comes the sweet refrain: "The blood of Jesus Christ, His Son, cleanseth us from all sin."

Do you who hear these assurances accept the sacrifice on Golgotha for yourself in humility and with deep gratitude, singing with devout but trembling lips:

> "In my hand no price I bring,
> Simply to Thy cross I cling."

Or if you care not for yourself, can you forget the kindly pleading? "Suffer the children to come unto me, and forbid them not." Would you risk to challenge God to curse your children, by withholding from them, or turning them against the Living Christ?

So be it, then! Together with Christians everywhere let us confess without apology or reservation:

> "Jesus' blood and righteousness
> My glory is and spotless dress."

The people sought a curse—God sent a benediction.

This is Calvary's Answer.

IV. SORROW AND JOY

The angels say unto her, Woman, why weepest thou? She saith unto them, Because they have taken away my Lord, and I know not where they have laid him. And when she had thus said, she turned herself back, and saw Jesus standing, and knew not that it was Jesus. . . . Jesus saith unto her, Mary. She turned herself, and saith unto him, Rabboni; which is to say, Master. John 20. 13, 14, 16.

CAN you see that disconsolate figure, Job, sitting among the ashes? Once he had been a merchant prince—now he was a broken man, ruined by adversity. Once popular and influentialtial—now left alone, forsaken, with no one to comfort, to encourage, or to cheer him. The world that he had builded by his own efforts, skill and industry, had crashed around him. Gone were his wealth, his esteem, his friends. Even his wife, from whom he had a right to expect support and comfort, taunted him by asking sarcastically: Are you still holding fast to your integrity? But Job had not lost *hope*. Yes, he still trusted in God.

Today we have presented to us the picture of a woman, just a plain woman. Perhaps even less than that. She had enjoyed the wonderful comfort of Christ's friendship. In spite of her sinful life, which had probably made her an outcast from polite society, she had found anchorage and a new hope in Jesus of Nazareth. Now her hope was crushed. Can anyone adequately depict the soul-agony of Mary Magdalene, as she wandered in the garden—alone, aimlessly? It was very early. She had not slept all night. Three times she reveals the agony of her heart, the cause of her tears, in the plaintive, pleading words: They have taken away my Lord! Will you please tell me where I can find him?

Out of the dim past we hear another voice. It is that of a king. And when a soul is in distress, it matters not whether it is hidden under royal robes or a peasant's garb. Can you sympathize with David in his sorrow when he confesses: "Out of the *depths* have I cried unto thee, O Lord. Lord, hear my voice—for with Thee there is forgiveness." Long before that hymn was written, Mary could sing: "Chief of sinners though I be, Jesus shed His blood for me." How she needed Him now! Her only friend! In her loneliness she could repeat her Master's pitiful cry: "Why hast thou forsaken me?"

Can you conceive of a greater sorrow than
to have lost your last and only hope? It is sad
enough never to have known Christ, but to have
had Him and *lost* Him is an even greater tragedy.
Tell me, has anyone or anything in your life ever
taken away or threatened to take away your
Christ? Have you ever read an article or a book
which has caused you to doubt His divinity? Have
you ever heard a sermon which left you wondering whether you can or should believe what the
Bible tells us? Have you ever had an experience
which has shaken your faith? Have you ever listened to a lecture or a philosophy, spun out of the
mind of man and not woven in and around the
mind of God, which ridiculed what you held
sacred and believed?

As a nation and as individuals we seem to be
slowly emerging from economic depression. Economic bankruptcy is distressing. To lose our
earthly possessions—have them swept away and
leave us poor and needy is discouraging. Spiritual bankruptcy is infinitely *worse*. To lose our
hold on eternal verities, to have our hopes blight-
ed, our faith shattered—these are losses which
make us poor indeed. When we suffer material
loss, we begin to think of causes, we analyze the
reasons, we face our mistakes, hoping to correct
them. Perhaps we have been careless with our
treasures and possessions; perhaps we have used
them unwisely. We take inventory. We see it
now! Are we equally concerned about our spiritual possessions to guard them carefully, to use

them profitably, to restore what may have been lost?

The Church is called the Bride of Christ—a woman, loved and wooed and won by the Son of God. Has she always remained true to her spouse? Tell me, is it still true that

> "The Church's one foundation
> Is Jesus Christ, the Lord?"

Is this age of materialism and rationalism replacing the Christ of Good Friday and Easter with a merely human hero, who corresponds to the yardstick of human intellect and reason? Is the cornerstone of the Christian church being chiseled out and only a hollow substitute offered? There was a time when many a church steeple carried on its tip as a weather vane the image of a fish. The Greek word fish has five letters, the initials of the names Jesus Christ, Son of God, Saviour. How significant and eloquent a confession! Today this symbol is very rarely seen, and, if it appears here and there, is probably never understood. The cross is the symbol of Christianity. And who will say that it is not eminently appropriate. What wonderful hymns have been written with the cross as their theme!

But what is the cross? An ornament? A thing of beauty? A work of art? An adornment? The cross is the deathbed of Christ! If it is anything less than that it loses its significance for the Christian. Some years ago I was visiting in a large and fashionable church. Among the rich appointments was a gorgeously tooled cross on the altar. Close examination revealed that at one time it had born the image of the Saviour. To the question why the image had been removed the answer was, that some members thought the cross would be more beautiful without the figure of a suffering, agonizing body. A cross from which Christ has been removed! Has that any significance? Must the Christian church sorrowfully lament with Mary: "They have taken away my Lord, and I know not where they have laid him"? Let those who deny the Easter miracle say what has become of the Christ. To the Christian, Christ is a living Christ, "my Lord." He is more than that. He is Jesus, who was dead and buried and rose again to live and reign for all eternity. This is the Christ as we know Him from the Scriptures.

But this epochal day in the sorrowing Mary's life was destined to take a turn. Weeping may endure for a night, but joy cometh in the morning, is God's promise to His children. A tremendous surprise was in store for her. Her crushing sorrow was to be dissolved in inexpressible joy. She saw a man standing, but did not recognize him. A voice with sweet tenderness called her by name: "Mary." The scales fell from her eyes. "Rabboni" she responds, and dedicates her life to His service.

Have any of you ever experienced a Gethsemane of your own? Crushed by a great sorrow, afflicted with doubts, which haunted you and gave you no rest or peace; seeking for something you could not find; waiting and hoping against hope; almost despairing, ready to give up everything? Then, unexpectedly, there would come a light through the gloom. The shadows of sorrow would be dispelled. The fog of uncertainty would be lifted; the faith to which you clung with desperation would be triumphant! Then, perhaps, you can understand in a small way Mary's joy on thta memorable morning. As she hastened to tell others of her discovery, to share with those others her joy, it echoed and re-echoed in her like wild pulsebeats: "He lives." It was Easter in Mary's heart. Not the date, not the flowers, not the sunshine, but the ringing conviction born of faith: He, my Saviour, was dead, but now lives. In and with Him, I, too, will live.

V. WHAT THINK YE OF CHRIST

While the Pharisees were gathered together, Jesus asked them, saying, What think ye of Christ? Whose son is he? Matthew 22. 42.

THIS question was asked two thousand years ago. An answer was given, so simple and direct that a child can understand it. And it came from the most reliable source—an undisputed authority—from Jesus Himself.

It is not strange that Jesus was the most discussed person of His time and generation. Both what He taught and preached as well as the

works He performed had caused a sensation.
Time and again it is recorded that His fame
spread throughout the land and even into the
neighboring countries. The things he said and
did made people wonder and think. "What thing
is this?" they said to one another. "What new
doctrine is this? Where does He get the power?"
Everywhere they flocked to Him and followed
Him from place to place. He became a public figure. He attracted the attention of the intellectu-
als; the political leaders became inerested; and
the religious authorities were plainly alarmed.
No one could be neutral and few, if any, were
willing to say they did not care. With this atmos-
phere of wonder and uncertainty all around Him,
for the sake of those few who remained true to
Him despite the unfavorable outlook, He puts a
question which served to bring the discussion into
the open and also to clarify the issue for all time.
"Who do men say that I, the Son of Man, am?"
he asked His disciples on one of those intimate
occasions when He would strengthen their waver-
ing faith. They had a ready answer because they
had heard people everywhere discuss Him. Some
say you are John the Baptist, some Elias, and
others Jeremias, or one of the prophets. Every-
body seemed to have some kind of opinion. Then,
without comment or denial as to what the general
public said, He strikes home, piercing their innermost souls with the searching question: "But
who say *ye*, that I am?" Like a flash of lightning
in the midst of a storm, clear and distinct, dis-

pelling every shadow of doubt, comes the answer from the spokesman of His disciples, *"Thou art the Christ, the Son of the living God."* What a confession, especially for that time and situation! How it must have cheered His heavy heart! If at least a few accepted Him for what He really was it made it easier for Him to set His face steadfastly toward Jerusalem. His sacrifice would not be in vain. I believe Jesus must have had a smile on His kindly face when He said to Peter: "Blessed art thou, Simon, for flesh and blood has not revealed it unto thee, but my Father, which is in heaven." That faith is heavenborn and those who possess it must cherish it as a gift of God.

The Pharisees also were given the opportunity to express themselves. To the direct question: "What think ye of Christ? Whose son is he?" they, too, give a clear and concise answer: "The Son of David." Right! But is that all? It is only half the truth. When Jesus pressed them to acknowledge more, they could not or would not commit themselves. Their answer did not include a living faith.

No case, however, is complete without a statement from the accused. Jesus Himself takes the witness stand. This was the crucial moment of His career. His future, His very life depended on His testimony. What did He claim for Himself? The scene was tremendously impressive. All the civic and religious leaders were present. Clothed with the dignity of his office, the high priest arises and puts Him under oath: "I adjure

thee by the living God, that thou tell us whether
thou be the Christ, the Son of God." Jesus answered with equal dignity: "Thou hast said, I
am." That was a sensational claim. They could
hardly believe their ears. It was just what they
needed and hoped for to condemn Him to death.
But they wanted to be doubly sure. Perhaps they
discussed it among themselves all night, for we
are told that the next morning all the high priests,
the scribes, and the elders of the people, together
with all the council, assembled once more. They
called Jesus in and again probed Him with the
two all-important questions: "Art thou the
Christ? Tell us. Art thou the Son of God? Tell
us." And again we hear His testimony of Himself: "Ye say that I am." With that His doom
was sealed. The verdict was: "He deserves
death."

But does that close the case? Is the testimony
all in? Are there any other witnesses who should
be heard? What do *you* say—and I? Have you
ever faced the compelling fact that in all honesty
we have only one alternative—either Jesus is all
and everything that He claimed for Himself, or
He is an imposter. There is no middle ground.
You and I must be either completely and wholly
for Him, or we are against Him. There can be
no neutrality in our attitude toward Christ. Or
can you think of any other choice? Shall the
Christian creed be revised to bring it into harmony with modern thinking or shall it be kept in
harmony with divine revelation?

As in that day, the minds of men today do not seem to be satisfied. Jesus is still a stumbling block and rock of offense" as was prophesied. Can you recall how the aged Simeon, when he held Him in his arms as a babe, said to His mother Mary: "This child is set for the fall and rising again of many—and for a sign which shall be spoken against." Will you weigh carefully the tremendous import of the statement of Christ Himself after He had spoken to the priests and elders the parable of the husbandmen who slew the son and heir: "Whosoever shall fall on the stone shall be broken: but on whomsoever it shall fall, it will grind him to powder." Today, as then, men are divided. To some He is only a prophet— one of many; to others, a great *religious leader*— one of many, who takes his place alongside of Mohammed and Buddha. To many He is the Great Physician who was and is yet concerned chiefly about the physical health and well-being of mankind. To a still larger group He is predominantly a great Teacher, ranking with Plato, Aristotle, and Socrates. He is claimed by any party or cult, if it happens to suit their purpose. The learned scholars rationalize over Him; philosophers draw distorted pictures; religious leaders quarrel and disagree, deny and affirm—and the man on the street *wonders*. Is it not strange that there should be such confusion and disagreement about Christ, when there is *only one authoritative* source of knowledge and information about Him — the Bible? Today, as never before in this generation,

the invitation, if not the challenge, goes out to
everyone who is hunting for a firm foundation to
stand on, who is groping for a reliable anchorage,
who longs for a hope to embrace—be he master or
disciple, bond or free, teacher or pupil, rich or
poor, of high station or lowly estate—"Search the
scriptures; for . . . *they* testify of me." The
difficulty, however, is not so much to discover
who Christ is or what Christ is; it rather centers
around the thought: Who and what is Christ *to
me?*

The question still stands, and not one of us can
successfully evade or avoid it: Whom say *ye* that
I am? The Christian believer has only one answer. It is simple and direct, but has in it the
exuberant ring of a joyful discovery and conviction: "Thou art the Christ, the Son of the
Living God, my Saviour!" Is that your answer?

The Imperative God

THEODORE HEIMARCK

THE IMPERATIVE GOD

I. God Is

THE introit for yesterday included the words, "Mine eyes are ever toward the Lord" and, "O my God, I trust in Thee." Since the first word in the Latin *introit* is *oculi*, the Sunday is often given this name, which translated reads *eyes*.

No one will dispute the importance of eyes, nor, I think, the influence which they exert on our character and being. In fact a good test of the inner man is to discover what the physical eyes seek out during seeing hours. If you can ascertain what a man is looking at, you will be pretty sure to know what he is looking for in life. It is natural, therefore, that the introit should speak about trusting in God—natural because we were first told that eyes were turned toward the Lord.

"Eyes toward the Lord" would be an excellent theme for whatever is said this week at these noonday services. And many of us find something distinctly refreshing in looking toward the Lord.

NOTE. During the preparation of these sermons Dr. Heimarck sought to follow the trend of religious thought through the medium of a standard popular periodical, *The Forum* being chosen as fitting the requirements. He desires to express his appreciation to its publishers for their courtesy in permitting the use of material from its pages. He extends thanks also to the *North American Review*, the *Christian Century*, Charles Scribner's Sons, and Little, Brown and Company for permission to make certain quotations from their publications.

As we stand gazing at His reality, we are overwhelmed again by His majesty, holiness, purposefulness, glory, and love. With new emphasis we confess with the whole Christian church, "I believe in God!"

Of course all of us have been saying this right along in our Sunday worship. Too often, though, we have followed it up by looking long and intently at self and its needs and desires. We even forget at times that our religion begins with God, and our faith, too. Our blessed Lord taught us to pray, "*Thy* kingdom come. *Thy* will be done." The suggestion here is pointed—God is doing something and willing something. Following the example of our Lord, we ought to make our personal desires and needs conform to this larger action and will, or else discard and abandon them. That this has not always been done by members of the church is seen by the criticism of one man who points out that honesty ought to compel us to substitute *my* for *thy*. The prayer would then be, "*My* kingdom come. *My* will be done." That comment cuts deep—it says that we are guilty of forgetting the very first commandment, "Thou shalt love the Lord thy God with all thy heart, soul, strength, and mind." One can not help but wonder what would happen if every prayer seeking selfish ends should suddenly be swallowed up in the vastness of a "not my will, but Thine be done." Certainly no greater confusion can be imagined than to think of millions of individuals selfishly praying *my*, receiving an-

swers strictly according to requests. Certainly
no greater harmony can be imagined than to think
of millions praying *thy* and finding happiness
and satisfaction in God's eternal and purposeful
will.

It does not seem possible to escape any longer
the fact that we have been guilty of distorting
God into a servant that waits upon our every
whim and fancy. It is a good thing, therefore,
that men the world over have arisen to point once
more to His majesty and Godhead, and to assert
positively that *God is*.

Not until we have accepted this as an assumption for life will we appreciate and take delight
in such passages of Scripture as: "The heavens
declare the glory of God, and the firmament
showeth his handiwork," "The Lord is my Shepherd," or "Give unto the Lord the glory due unto
his Name; worship the Lord in the beauty of
holiness." Ah! when will we recover the vision
these lines portray? Not, methinks, until we are
ready to stand with our eyes toward God.

Not until then, either, will we know the horror
of sin. Long ago one man made confession saying, "Against thee have I sinned and done this
evil in thy sight." Take away the *thee* and the
thy, and sin vanishes. Unless the *Is*-ness and
Holiness of God stares us in the face, we fail to
comprehend the tragedy of living at odds and
cross-purposes with Him. If we have lost the consciousness of sin, as so many say, it must be be-

cause we have first lost the consciousness of a
living God.

That is why I want to utilize my time this week
to witness to a God that was and is and ever shall
be. Just now, during this sober Lenten season,
is an opportune time to tear our gaze from traffic
and commotion, and center it on God.

To do this we are not going to enter into lengthy
argumentation. We are not going to try to show
the reasonableness of Him. But once more we are
going to witness to a God that has a plan for
eternity—a God that is building the Eternal City.
And those of you who have become the victims
of the bedlam of this life, its confusion, its mean-
inglessness, its fears, anxieties, sin, and shame,
ought to ask yourselves again and again whether
you are certain you have understood the meaning
and implication of the Christian's God. The
church declares that God has a plan and will
carry it through to completion, and that this plan
includes you. Do you not see that the claim of the
church is that life and all things were meant for
Him? That to create a different plan and purpose
for yourself is sheer folly? That you can not im-
pose your scheme upon a plan that is from eternity? That His plan is woven into the very fabric
of all existence? When you accept this, and when
you begin to live on these assumptions, you will
understand and share that untroubled trust and
confidence so characteristic of all His true children, and of His Son, even Christ Jesus.

But if you are to live this kind of life, you will

have to take time to stand with your eyes toward the Lord. You will have to go aside from the turmoil and stress of life and receive assurance from God Himself. Moses did just that.

Remember how Moses saw a burning bush and went aside to investigate? Bear in mind the promise, "If you truly seek me, ye shall surely find." The barefooted and questioning Moses found a God that declared, *I am.* He surrendered finally to that timeless God, lived out his life as though God was . . . and He was. I like that *I-am God.* There is something so perpetual and eternal about Him—something so solid on which to live and move and have my being, and something so overwhelmingly great. And you will find, too, as you stand barefooted (reverently) and questioning (seeking), that He will answer and will renew your strength; "ye shall mount up with wings as eagles; ye shall run and not be weary; and ye shall walk, and not faint." It will put the song of Sidney Lanier's "The Marshes of Glynn" in your heart of new hope and confidence:

"As the marsh hen secretly builds on the watery sod,
  Behold I will build me a nest on the greatness of God;
  I will fly in the greatness of God as the marsh hen flies
  In the freedom that fills all the space twixt the marsh
        and the skies;
  By so many roots as the marsh grass sends in the sod
  I will heartily lay me a-hold of the greatness of God."

Oh, if only you could get at the knowledge that *God is,* and tread your way back into the busy life with optimism and fearless confidence and a song of praise to God on your lips. What a witness that would be to the world that God matters! The world desperately needs such witnessing from Christians. Mankind is on the march again, looking for some vital truth to give itself to.

It is not difficult to prove this new day of opportunity. Most of you can remember the trend of the last decade. Ten years ago we were reading in popular magazines about the faults of the church, its ministry, and its message. Unbounded confidence was placed in man to rule and rule well. Probably the most blatant of this school of thought was the same H. L. Mencken who was written about recently in the *North American Review*.[1] The author finds that "America's Bad Boy" is "a cropper at literary criticism," "betrays little understanding of the historical church," is a "poser as an authority in a wide variety of subjects," and is a man "who solved the depression by denying it."

There can be no question but what the philosophy of this school is all but gone, and that a new searching note is emerging. Six years ago we were shocked to read "Revolt from Cynicism," and it was daring to write, "I'm Going Back to Church, and So Are Thousands of Others," and in order, mind you, "to achieve that inner contentment so many old-fashioned Christians seem to possess but which is rather conspicuously lacking in the ranks of the intelligentsia." And these articles were followed by "Science Changes Its

---

[1] Winter Issue, 1938-1939, *Mencken Twilight*, by Charles Angoff.

Mind," "A Minister's Day," and "An Unbeliever Goes to Church." In 1934 Pearl S. Buck dares herald a day when "It seems the latest independence in poets and others is to try God for a change. . . . Religion, in short, is in again. The churches are filling once more."[2] The past couple of years we have been reading about how to make friends with ourself, and about complexes and fears. It is plainly evident that man has lost faith in himself and his ability to shape and mold the world about him. There is a hunger for spiritual values, and a desire to find something eternal and purposeful.

With this kind of picture before us, you can understand why I count it so urgent that you and I have a *living* God to share with the world around us. You can understand, too, why the first thing I want to do is to confront you with the fact of God. For it is up to you, you who are interested enough to come to such services as this one today, to point the way to the thousands around you—to name the unnamed hunger of restless souls as God-hunger. It is up to you to devoutly pray and zealously work to the end that God's kingdom may come and God's will be done. "Be not afraid," said the Lord to Paul, "but speak, and hold not thy peace: For I am with thee, and

[2] THE FORUM: *Revolt from Cynicism*, Dawn Lovelace, May, 1932; *I'm Going Back to Church*, Anonymous, July, 1932; *Science Changes Its Mind*, Waldemar Kaempffert, August, 1933; *A Minister's Day*, Charles J. Dutton, September, 1933; *An Unbeliever Goes to Church*, Norman Hapgood, November, 1933; *It's Convenient to Worship God*, Pearl S. Buck, October, 1934.

no man shall set on thee to hurt thee: for I have
much people in this city."

Eyes toward the Lord, then, not only this week
but evermore. Eyes toward the Lord because His
way is the way of purpose and peace. Eyes
toward the Lord because He would fain build His
kingdom using your hands and your testimony.
Amen.

II. The God of Jesus

THE meditation yesterday centered on the fact
of God. We tried simply to declare His reality.
The conclusion to the whole matter was that we
as Christians face the responsibility of sharing
a real God with a bewildered people—a responsibility that is not properly shouldered until we
know His reality and willingly build lives on this
living God who declares, I AM.

There is a dearth of knowledge about God.
This is the disappointing thing many of us experience even among people who presume to call
themselves Christians. There are plenty of people
who know something about Jesus, and many of
them have a very sweet faith in Him, but somehow they have completely missed the point that
Jesus came to reveal the Father. It is a mistake,
we think, to say that He came to teach a morality
or a sociology only—or at all. We fail miserably
to understand our blessed Lord's life and teaching
if we do not grasp that here was God's will in
action—a revelation, therefore, of God's intent,

purpose, plan, and nature. What else could He mean when He plainly said, "Ye that have seen me have seen the Father"? The common mistake is to stop at Jesus and overlook His revelation. The result is a blend of sentiment and morality that is far from the truth. The God of Jesus was a God with a will. That will Jesus accepted as authoritative and final. His victories were victories because He bowed to that will. His "follow me" must mean to follow Him there, too. It is very plain that Jesus had an I-AM God, and that the I-AM God is the God of Jesus.

In spite of the fact, however, that there is a very definite plainness about the God of Jesus, there is also a great deal which is very mysterious and vague. And any God that is presented to the world today as the God of Jesus must be as plain and as mysterious as this.

He must be as plain as this because of the tendency to satisfy the mood of religion with a very vague God. The popular distortion of noble mysticism is one such attempt to satisfy God-hunger in the soul. The "Return to Religion" will lose its charm if no one can point with certainty to a real God. The novelty of a God-feel will wear off. I doubt if quiet music, beautiful services and the thrill of being lifted heavnward, though I love it all, can be a successful substitute for really knowing God. These things must follow a sound knowledge of and a sturdy faith in God. We must learn to know the God of a sane mind, and meet Him with out whole person alive to His Being.

On the other hand, He must be as vague as the God of Jesus, because God, if He is to actually be God, must exceed the possibilities of human definitions and wisdom. It is impossible, therefore, for me to believe that rationalism will ever be able to arrive at God or bring a united witness—there certainly have been plenty of test flights and ample time—they have not lacked either courage or opportunity. And yet when they return with such tremendous discoveries as that God must be an "idea," or simple "goodness," or "value," or "yourself," or "change," I—well, I throw up my hands in despair and hold the closer to the God of Jesus. He is far more understandable and far more mysterious. Some one said that "every rationalist is his own clubfooted God"—I am beginning to see depths of wisdom there. The charge of wishful thinking, hurled so often at the church, can safely be hurled back, and defiantly, at every and all rationalists.

So I am left with no alternative, and revelation becomes more than a way of knowing God—it becomes the only way. If you accept this, the revelation which we have in Christ Jesus becomes a very natural way as well as a supernatural one. Now I suspect that some one will accuse me of falling a victim to Barthianism and others will find this the sound Lutheran position, and personally I care not a whit what you find—I prefer, though, to have you find and call this the knowledge of the God of Jesus.

We come very early to this knowledge in the

life of our Lord. He was twelve years old and in the temple—anxious parents find Him and are met by His puzzled and sturdy "Knew ye not that I must be about my Father's business?" Whoever said that the boy put his question wistfully did not know his twelve-year-olds—puzzled it may have been—and certainly sturdy, but never wistful. The startling thing is that He meant it—always for Jesus there was a "Father's business." "My Father worketh," He later said; and no one can read His story without gathering that the I-AM God of Jesus is an active God—a God that is engaged in doing something. And all of Scripture, all of history, all of experience tells us that the work this God is at is the work of creation.

The more we think of Him as the Creator, the more we think of Him as Genius. In this world of ours, you know, we often say of this or that man that he is a genius. We mean by that, do we not, that this person has a gift which is his in superabundance. The quantity and quality of this gift varies in man—it is never pure. The genius of God, if He is like that, is absolute genius and pure. Now all genius is alike in one respect— that is, they make room for their genius at any cost and their very existence seems to depend upon the opportunity and freedom to express it. A painter genius, for instance, must paint at any price. What cares he for public approval or even remuneration? It is enough that he has opportunity to express his genius and create things for the sheer joy of expression. The fact is that to such a one days, weeks, and months are as nothing—food, clothes, and shelter are as nothing—the only passion of life is to create according to the measure of genius. God must be like that. More, of course, than the kind of thing we call genius, but that and more—pure genius. His is a talent which is not of the earth, but divine. We can not measure it, nor even rightly name it, but if we must try, we will say that He is like that. We will declare, too, that the world and all that is therein is a part of such genius or the result of it—that God could not avoid creating for it was His very nature to create and the only really satisfying thing He could do.

Earlier in the discussion we pointed out the submission of Jesus to a Will. We declare now that God is Creator—Genius—Will. This means to us that what has been done and what is being done is executed by will and mind. Creation is a meaningful thing: a thing not only set in motion but governed and guided to very definite ends. God's creation is still in the process of completion. That is why Jesus talked about a work to be done, and that is why we can have a part in His business. To become a part of His plan and His way and His business is to understand the true significance of the I-AM God. It is easy to understand, therefore, why Waldemar Kaempffert should write that "the mechanical universe is gone"—why should it not go? It had no meaning. Madame Chiang Kai-Shek is understood, too, when she writes, "With me religion is a very simple thing. It means to try with all my heart and soul and strength and mind to do the *will* of God [italics my own]. I feel that God has given we a work to do for China. . . . At this time of writing, I am with my husband in the heart of the bandit area. Constantly exposed to dangers, I am unafraid. I know that nothing can happen either to the General or to me till our work is done. After that, what does it matter?"[1]

Of course, "what does it matter?" as long as she and we are going with life and not fighting it—as long as there is a destiny and purpose. In short, God has a plan, and will carry it through. Gamaliel was right, "If this thing be of God, no one can hinder it." God's will, you see, is actually done without us or our prayer, "Thy will be done," and is the only possible answer to the "whys" of all ages. "What is this great mechanism," writes William Allan White,[2] "that moves and guides events, roughhews destiny, shapes careers to fit the times? Finger the puzzle, fondle it, shake it up, pore over it as you will, O Philosopher! In the end, with all your lore and learning, you can only say with the idle and the blind, God knows!" Yes, but God does know. And even as Jesus prayed, "Thy will be done," so we are prepared to pray. We doubt not but what it will be a difficult road at times, but we will walk it as best we can because we know that life runs only that way. It is very plain that to rebel at His plan is to

---

[1] THE FORUM, *"What Religion Means to Me,"* Madame Chiang Kai-Shek, March, 1934.
[2] WILLIAM ALLAN WHITE, *"Masks in a Pageant."*

invite disaster. The Old Testament as well as the New is replete with illustrations of this folly—the Old Testament tells them a bit too vividly to suit the sweet-tempered higher critics, but it does tell them. And so out to life we go, supremely confident that it is His will and His plan that matters, ready to pray "Thy will be done," and read to be co-workers with Him in the greatest enterprise ever conceived—that of building the eternal kingdom of God.

III. GOD'S DETERMINATIVE LOVE

THE Christian church with one accord testifies that God is love. No one dares deny that the God of Jesus was just that. Our blessed Lord never lost faith in the love of His Father. Strange, too, that He did not, when you stop to think about it. His life was one of poverty, of sorrow (He wept, you know, over Jerusalem), of suffering, of being bitterly hated and utterly forsaken. Many people, with a single experience as acrimonious and painful as this, would be quick to question the fact of God's love. Jesus did not. He prayed, and taught His followers to pray, "Our Father." If we knew the secret of such confident trust in God as love, we would have an answer for those who constantly ask, "How can God be love when He permits poverty, sickness, hatred, and dying?" And if we had this answer, we could help many earnest seekers for truth, as well as effectively silence those who sit in the scorner's seat.

Not a little misunderstanding could be avoided if it were possible to give this love a name which would immediately distinguish it from the associations of common usage. Too often it is used to describe a passing whim or violent feeling. The church never intended that it should become confused and limited by such first cousins as "like," "attachment," "fancy," "admiration," or "infatuation." God's love is made of sturdier stuff than this—it has the steel of will in it.

A little boy stole out into a kitchen one day and took an eight-ounce bottle of cough medicine. He drank it down like pop. The father called the doctor and was told to keep the boy awake for awhile with coffee and chatter. For hours the father very cruelly kept a drowsy three-year-old from sleep which he begged for; afraid, you see, that the lad might sleep away, the victim of an overdose of morphine. That was not "infatuation," nor "fancy," nor "admiration," nor even ordinary manifestation of "liking," but it was love.

But even this illustration, and dozens like it, fails to define the love of God. It transcends, of course, the limitations of definition, but it is never rightly understood until allowance is made for the steel of love. And by that we mean that quality in love which interests itself in ultimate objectives and ultimate values—indeed, often pays a heavy price to attain and achieve them.

A thing that might help us, therefore, is to study anew God's objectives and try to discover His sense of ultimate values. Such a study must be centered on man.

Nothing in all creation is quite as wonderful as man. Nothing is quite as mysterious as man. There he stands, a bundle of muscle, tissue, flesh, bone, held together with skin. There he stands, a bundle of nerves, thoughts, desires, hopes, fears, longings, and ideals. What is he good for? Why is he? Is there a plan?

The church, and only the church, is ready to assure you that there is a plan. We suppose you know the story well. We remind you, however, of it, and invite you to think about it.

Remember how we thought yesterday about the Creator-Genius God? Well, when I think about man, I see this Creator-Genius at work and imagine, at least, that man constituted a real problem. There was with God a vision of sharing creation with a soul—a thing that could love and respond to love. Here was a glorious vision of a free being—free to think, free to plan, free to choose, free to love. God saw evil as a real danger—"suppose they use their freedom for that, and I know they will." What should God do? Would you have Him make a being less than He was able? God could not do that—He had to be true to His Creator-Genius. He had to create according to that genius—His very nature demanded it. So man was given his freedom—free to love Him, free to worship Him, free to glorify

Him, free to build His kingdom and complete the plan. God, knowing well the suffering that would follow, endured that suffering in order that His love might not do less than love dictated. From eternity God set a cross on a hillside and vowed that He would finish His creation according to the heighth, and breadth, and depth of His love. By ceaseless suffering toil, by revelation, and by treading the earth of man, God determined to win man for Himself as planned by Himself. There would be, some day, perfected creation—there would be free man freely choosing Him, and freely loving, freely worshiping, freely glorifying Him. Not slaves, but free. No robots, but sons. And God said, "When man sees His God, when he sees how life could be and should be lived, when he sees how I give myself for him, when he sees how I share my victory with him, then man will find his life by giving it away."

That plan has gathered thousands under the banner of the cross. Still we fail to understand it, but we catch a little of its meaning—enough to know that suffering, pain, and dying is a poor price, indeed, to pay for the glorious right of being a free man, and freely loving God, and freely worshiping Him, and freely serving Him— how else could we be sons and not machines? Whenever I see human wreckage, I see a suffering God, but a God content to suffer in order that man might be man. Every piece of human wreckage, as well as every Christ-lover, eloquently witnesses to the love of God. Love that could not create less than love demanded.

The absolute limit of that love is seen in the cross. God could not exceed that without being untrue to love. And so there, just there, is God's determinative love. There is the sword that shall divide the world of man—there is the final judge of who will find life's ultimate meaning and purpose.

Will man find his answer here? His satisfaction? His victory and freedom? Some will. Yes, many will. This world of man is beginning to discover that life is more than food and clothing, and is weary of defeat. Defeat because man thrust man where God ought to be—at the heart of the universe. Defeat because man thought he was strong enough for life, and strong enough to order life. But slowly it is beginning to dawn upon his consciousness that life lived in rebellion at God's purpose and plan can only come to nought. Man though that freedom meant freedom to indulge the appetites of the flesh and to satisfy the lust and the pride of life. He is not sure of this any more. In fact many are ready to admit that this freedom is a sad mistake—that it actually is not freedom at all. Some are ready to say that they are slaves, not free. "It becomes plain," writes one man, "that the idea that we are 'free' has been more than an intellectual error. It is an idea that has deceived and jaded us, physically as well as spiritually. In spite of all our novelists and all our sentimental liberals and all the Bertrand Russells in the world, the Puritan is still very much alive."[1] And the Puritan, in this case, is the law of life. Life is a one-way lane.

This seems to be further substantiated when we read another article entitled, "I Thought I Was Modern." The author writes, "What is called free love exacts payment to the uttermost farthing in the most precious coinage in the world—self-esteem, self-confidence, honesty, integrity, health, and peace of mind. Modern? So were we. Gallant, too, and courageous, if you will—but doomed."[2] And Winfred Rhodes tells of one individual who suffered headache, fear, exhaustion, attacks of coughing, loss of appetite, and loss of weight because of an early sin. The result was a feeling of guilt and fear. Another writer tells us, "When spirit is defective, there enter all sorts of fears—fear of death and damnation, fear of war, fear of loss of income, fear of the dark."

You see, evil spirits are back to haunt us. Man thought he was through with evil spirits and conscience, and gloried in his freedom, and now he discovers he is a slave to evil spirits that torment his peace of mind and work havoc with his body. To be sure, he does not call it sin now—not yet—but will he not see, and soon, that it makes very little difference whether he calls it inner fears, conflicts, feel of guilt, inhibitions, or the rest of

---

[1] THE FORUM, "The Puritan Still Walks," John Hyde Preston, Feb., 1932.

[2] THE FORUM, "I Thought I Was Modern," Evelyn Havens, Oct., 1936.

the psycho jargon, or just plain sin? And is it not all the evidence of souls restless and uneasy because they have lost the way? And is it not time to shout that where sin abounds, there does the grace of God much more abound? Surely we must see that inner harmony is not achieved save as it reconciles self to self's purpose—to belong freely to God.

And so you see the cross is judging us again. The cross is saving us again—saving us from slavery to liberty—saving us from aimlessness to purposefulness—saving us from stoic endurance to a victorious understanding of God's suffering love. Can God be love? The cross shouts back, "Yes." Men of all ages, saints and martyrs of the church, all those who have found that God's plan is to create truly free beings through the cross—all these shout back, "Yes."

IV. MAN'S ALTERNATIVE

THE call today is to think about man's alternative. Now in one sense man has no alternative. That is, man has a God whether he likes it or not, and whether he knows it or not, and whether he chooses or not. By God we mean that which a man worships, fears, loves, and trusts. Such a definition, and a good one it is, allows no choice but to have a God. The thing which man counts worthy of his life, spends his time with, and upon which he lavishes his interest and devotion, and

depends upon and trusts in as the source of all his
joy and strength, that is his God. Some folks
flatter themselves into believing that they can live
by a simple negative belief. No one lives by what
he denies—he really lives by what he believes.
Man may have several gods or may change gods,
but that which he counts worthy of his life and
trusts and reverences is a god. To deny one god
is to flee to another. It may not always be a conscious choice—like so many decisions along life's
way, we decide by not deciding. The human
heart has a throne and it is always occupied.
Man lives always by affirmations—not negations.

A typical instance of this thing is seen in
Cronin's "The Citadel," where it is said of Denny,
one of the characters, that "Denny's codex was
literally the opposite of everything which Manson
had been taught. Condensed and framed, it might
well have hung, textlike, above his bed: 'I do not
believe.' " But to read the novel is to understand
that Denny did not live by this negative. If he
had, he would not have been a character either in
a novel or in life. Denny lived by what he believed to be worth while in the medical profes-
sion—by a certain rugged honesty and poorly
concealed sentiment. That thing that Denny
called his highest good, the thing he trusted and
gave himself to, that was his god. Every one is
like Denny, for man always fills the chair in his
throne room.

It is quite plain that the alternative can not be
whether or not we shall have a god. The alterna-

tive is rather whether we will trouble ourselves sufficiently to intelligently select an occupant for the throne. That we ought to prod ourselves to active participation in the choice becomes clearer every day.

"Today, almost certainly, we are standing at a turning point in history." So writes Dr. Tittle in *The Christian Century,* November 9, 1938. "There is a road which leads to destruction; there is a road which leads to life—and none of us yet knows which of these roads mankind will take. . . . Fundamentally, the crisis which now confronts us is a spiritual crisis, having to do with our beliefs, our attitudes, our desires and ambitions. We are now called upon to decide whom we will serve. Shall it be other gods, such as race, nation, class, private interset? Or shall it be God, even the Father of our Lord Jesus Christ? . . . The dread horsemen that are now riding in Asia and threatening to ride over all the world are, it is interesting to note, the four horsemen of the Apocalypse—militarism, war, famine, and death. Why are they riding and threatening to ride? The answer, I believe, is given in this: 'Thou shalt have no other gods before me. . . . If ye worship other gods ye shall surely perish.' "

What Dr. Tittle wrote is actually finding expression in dozens of books and magazines. It is one more shock which is helping to jar loose our complacency. It is so startling because, you see, it seems to say that it does not matter what our neighbor serves as God. That is rather different from what we have been accustomed to think. It was our folly, too, to believe that the faith of others had no bearing on our own. And was it not almost taken for granted that it was an intrusion to question another man's belief? Every one said, "Now, of course, you have the right to believe your way, and all I ask is that you leave my faithlife alone." Everyone said, "What I believe is my personal problem." When it came to beliefs, therefore, every one hung out a "No Trespassing" sign—and no one even questioned the right to do so. It is almost laughable today—I mean the proportions to which we have distorted personal rights and liberties. But we did it—our faith went to church with us, came home, and was locked up in the china closet for another week. Now we realize that it does make a difference what our neighbor does with God and what gods they serve. We know that if the world selects force, force will rule. If it is wealth, wealth will rule. If it is pleasure, lust of the flesh will rule. Everyone knows that man tends to become more and more like what he worships. It is not secret any more, the fact that the fate of the world depends upon what god man will choose.

It needs hardly be said that Christians have a job on their hands. You who have chosen the God of Jesus, how many have you brought into His camp? You who are Christians, give an accounting of your stewardship. Do you not realize that not only your life, but the lives of your loved ones depend upon your activity to help the world decide about God? "Am I my brother's keeper?" Of course. The question, "Where is thy brother?" brings a flush of shame and a drooping head because we know we have acquiesced too readily in the spirit of our age. We did not understand the urgency of our Father's business. We did not understand that we would be called to account so soon for the stewardship of the "mysteries of God." We hardly believed that our sin would find us out.

If the truth must be known, we, the Christians, have sinned against the most holy and imperative God. Our religion has not been a conveyance, but a convenience—we have been conventionalists and not conversants. This is our shame, and here we begin reconstruction with repentance, the kind of repentance that carries with it the implication to mend our ways. If we are thus minded, we do well to begin by choosing deliberately a God for ourselves. Line up the gods and God— call the roll: when you get through, you will discover that the choice narrows down to only two. These two remain, as ever, the God of Jesus and the Devil's world. But choose one—the cross demands it.

God has always been demanding it. There was that day when Joshua and Moses came back to the camp only to find the people worshiping a golden calf. Moses took that calf and ground it to bits and poured the dust into the water—then strode out to the gate and called for a decision: "Who will be on the Lord's side?"—make up your mind which God you will choose. Then there was Joshua in his later years who called the people together and urged the decision anew upon them: "Who will be on the Lord's side?"—make up your minds now. There was Elijah crying to the people: "Make up your mind, will ye have Baal or the Lord?" Jesus came saying, "Ye can not serve God and mammon"—make your choice. And in Revelations we hear the indictment of that people who would be neither hot nor cold—make up your mind. Indecision, halting between the two, is unsavory. Decide something and consecrate yourself to that choice.

Naturally you will choose the God of Jesus. You can not do otherwise when compelled to choose. You want love, not hate. You want a world of brothers, not a world of hostile tribes and nations. You want unselfishness, not greed. You want honesty and integrity, not deceit and Iscariotism. You want the nobility of the individual soul-worth—and so, it will have to be the God of Jesus for you.

This is the choice you will have to make, not only today, but every day. Faith and trust and confidence will be strengthened and sustained only as you start out each day with firm decision. And, of course, you will have to change prayer habits. You will have to learn that the first lesson in prayer started with "Thy kingdom come," and "Thy will be done." Our Lord did not place first the "give us this day" or "deliver us from evil"— another lesson in putting first things first. The lesson, too, of the cross—"take up your cross" and go out on a lonely hill and put to death the self with its pride and selfishness. Let the new man daily arise and say, "Father, Thy will be done."

And why talk to you when a whole world must decide? Because you are the world—you and you and you. The only real hope for a world decision for the God of Jesus, is the hope that *you* will learn to say, "Thy" instead of "my." Let no one tell you that to so decide is an attempt to escape from reality—it is facing the reality of God and consciously choosing when whole multitudes are unsuspectingly having a god of this world thrust upon them.

V. God's Heaven

MORE than twenty-three hundred years ago, two pagan philosophers fell into a discussion of the problem of immorality. "It seems to me, Socrates," said the one, "that it is very difficult, if not impossible, in this present life to have clear knowledge concerning such subjects, but that, on the other hand, it is the mark of a faint-hearted spirit to desist from examining all that is said about them . . . or to abandon the search so long as there is any chance of light anywhere. For on such subjects one ought to secure one of two things, either to learn or discover the truth, or, if this is impossible, to get the best of human

argument and the hardest to refute, and relying
on this as on a raft, to sail the perilous sea of life;
unless one were able, more securely and less perilously, to make one's journey upon a safer vessel—
upon *some divine word*" [italics my own].

More than twenty-three hundred years later, a
man writes and says, "Yes, but—I am what I
am—I am a man, and therefore have immortal
longings in me. I did not put them there. They
are there. And science must take account of
them."[1] A woman writes: "All about me I felt
this ocean of life ready to overflow and crush
down and bury forever the nothingness of death.
I had seen too often the sun, shining after the
rain, lift the bent oat stalks toward the sky. I
had seen too often the maples flaming in March."[2]
Another writes: "It is not a fact that modern
man has no further use for religion. As long as
human love, affection, and sympathy are brought
up against the blank wall of suffering, frustra-
tion, and death, human beings will continue to
seek solace and peace in some inner fastness of
the self."[3]

These longings stand at either end of a bridge
spanning more than twenty-three hundred years.
Every one of those years has found human hearts
groping for the desired assurance that immortality is a fact. Looking backward over these
years is to find positive evidence that man is im-

---

[1] THE FORUM, *The Sixth Decade,* Lee Wilson Dodd, October, 1931.
[2] THE FORUM, *Can Prayer Be Answered?* May Austin, May, 1934.
[3] THE FORUM, *Science and Religion,* Boshi Sen, December, 1935.

mortal by nature—that is, that he has an urge for
immortality. That urge is prompted by the need
of finding completeness to life. Man says, "Where
shall I find completed love—never? Where shall
I find completed justice—never? Where shall I
find completed joy—never?" And those questions,
if the be answered with a "never," prompt another question: "Why, then, were these longings
placed within me, if they are never to find completion?" Surely it does seem rather unreasonable to believe that man's reach shall always exceed his grasp. Shall life end without achieving?

Now, with these desires, man must have done
considerable searching for the truth. If Socrates
and his friend should walk our streets again,
would they find much knowledge in the possession
of modern man which they did not possess? They
might, for instance, go to that great scientist of
our generation, Mr. Einstein. We know his answer, "Neither can I believe that the individual
survives the death of the body, although feeble
souls harbor such thoughts through fear of ridiculous egotism."[4] I can almost hear them put another question, "But Mr. Einstein, suppose it is
neither fear nor ridiculous egotism, but suppose
man is like the homing pigeon, and possesses a
mysterious 'secret of orientation, which gives it
the mastery of space'?" With that parting question, they might depart to pay another great scientist a visit. This time it will be Pasteur, the
father of modern bacteriology. To their question,

---

⁴ THE FORUM, *What I Believe*, Albert Einstein, October, 1930.

he would answer, "My philosophy is of the heart
and not of the mind, and I give myself up, for instance, to those feelings about eternity which
come naturally at the bedside of a cherished child
drawing its last breath. At those supreme moments there is something in the depths of our
souls which tells us that the world may be more
than a mere combination of phenomena proper
to a mechanical equilibrium brought out of
chaos." With that, they might stop before John
Quincy Adams at the age of eighty and say, "Good
morning, and how are you today?" Mr. Adams
would reply, "Thank you, John Quincy Adams is
well, sirs, quite well. . . . The house in which he
lives is becoming dilapidated. It is tottering upon
its foundation. Time has nearly destroyed it. Its
roof is pretty well worn out. Its walls are much
shattered and it trembles with every wind. The
old tenement is becoming almost unfit to live in
and I think John Quincy Adams will have to move
out soon. But John Quincy Adams is quite well,
sirs." With that, I believe these two pagan philosophers would wink at each other and say, "I
guess the old world still has the problem, and we
did not do so badly with it in our own day."

But suppose, then, the church bells should ring.
Suppose these two were to join the throngs of
worshipers, and see the people kneel in prayer
and sing joyous hymns about an Easter morning—and about "Now is Christ risen, the first
fruits of them that sleep." Would they remember
their conversation of twenty-three hundred years

ago? They had said one to another, "unless one were able, more securely and less perilously, to make one's journey upon a safer vessel—upon some *divine word*." Would they receive it?

Naturally we will never know what their answer would be. We do know that they desired that kind of assurance for the knowledge of the heart. There is that kind of knowledge, you know. We are beginning to respect it, too. In his book, *Solitude and Society*, Nicolas Berdyaev writes: "It is a prejudice to believe that knowledge is always rational, that there is no such thing as irrational knowledge. Actually, we apprehend a great deal more through feeling than by intellection; . . . the heart is the centre of the entire man."[5] And so, with a new respect for the veracity of the soul's language, we place the *urge* aboard the "safer vessel" of a *divine word*, and plan to live forever.

That "*Word* was made flesh and dwelt among us." We hear Him talk about "many mansions," and going to His Father. We see His whole life pointed toward eternity—toward God's heaven. "And if I go," He said, "I will come again," and, "because I live, ye shall live also." Then there was darkness lying heavy upon three crosses, there was crying and dying and a burial in a new tomb in a garden. Then there was a guard placed by the side of that tomb, and a stone rolled away on the third day, and folks were bribed to say

[5] Nicolas Berdyaev, *Solitude and Society*, Charles Scribner's Sons, N. Y., 1938.

that the disciples had stolen the body, and there
were reports after reports of His presence again.
Frenzied disciples met behind locked doors and
there was an Ascension and a Pentecost. Out of
the furor of those days disciples learned that
there was a victory in His defeat, and they were
constrained to preach and declare that victory
in the face of any and all kinds of opposition and
persecution. Ever since then, the church has been
ringing its bells, calling men together to declare
hope and meaning for life and eternity.

The first meaning is that God is still at work
completing His creation. The Creator God is
building His eternal city. Human wisdom can not
follow the plan—it is foolishness unto Him. "The
stone which the builders disallowed, the same is
made the head of the corner." Man builds with
steel and iron, canon and force—God builds with
a cross and love. Man builds with wood and
stone—God builds with human lives. "Ye are the
household of God, built upon the foundations of
the apostles and prophets, Jesus Christ himself
being the chief cornerstone; in whom all the
building fitly framed together groweth unto an
holy temple in the Lord: In whom ye also are
builded together for an habitation of God through
the Spirit." "To this end was I born," said Jesus—and for us, too, there is a "for this cause
was I born." Here, and here only, is man's destiny. You were meant to be a part of that building of God—to deny it is to deny meaning for life.

Foolishness? Yes, *divine foolishness*. Who other

than God could conceive of such a plan? A plan that calls for free man, freely loving Him, and freely serving Him, and freely glorifying Him. Who but God could conceive of building a kingdom of love? Who but God would think of building with the "foolishness of preaching"? Who but God would think of building out of failure and wreckage and suffering and dying?

But so it is. The cross in history declares it. The cross from eternity verifies it. The cross of today demands it. There is no meaning for the universe or for life save as it begins with God's plan and ends with God's heaven.

"I believe, help Thou mine unbelief"—so prayed one in the temple, and so pray I, for I know that "he that endures faithfully unto the end, to him will be given the crown of *life*."

Thus saith the Lord.   Amen.

The Demands of Love

J. ALLEN LEAS

THE DEMANDS OF LOVE

We love him, because he first loved us. 1 John 4. 19.

ALL first things come from God. New ideas, new discoveries, new life, new love, everything new comes from Him. He brought love to earth and taught men how to love. Our text suggests two loves: a greater and the smaller; His love and our love. He lays down the terms, and expects us, if we would be His, to sign on the dotted line. Somewhere we read: "Thou shalt love the Lord thy God with all thy heart and mind and soul." In the light of His great love it is something small and insignificant, this love of ours. His love is great and overshadowing. It is too deep and too broad for us to comprehend; we can catalog it but never measure it.

God first declared His love, then He practiced it, and then He said, Now that I have shown you how love acts, you, too, must love; you must love me, and you must love your neighbor. We may, therefore, mention: (1) *Love Declared;* (2) *Love Enacted;* and finally, (3) *Love's Demands.*

God declared that first love when He said: "When Israel was a child, I loved him." Again He said, "I have loved thee with an everlasting love." Many times in the New Testament the same love toward the whole human race is expressed in exact terms or in a multitude of ways no less clear or definite.

In the course of time, the great Lover proceeds to demonstrate His love in ways that can not be misunderstood. May we be permitted to suggest that He proceeds to enact His love upon the stage of the world, not indeed in make-believe, but as one bent upon most serious business. If the whole process can be considered as an *act*, we may with propriety speak of several scenes, in which certain details are worked out with beauty or at least with precision.

SCENE 1—A hut on the outskirts of a hamlet. A cattle stall. A chubby child, with laughter and smiles, such is the setting. There is no orchestra to play, but from afar there come strains sweeter than the music of earth. There is heard a voice speaking; not much is heard, but there is something about peace and goodwill on earth and among men.

SCENE 2—An open plain, fields of poppies and lilies; here and there a ravine and now and then a farmer sowing his little field. Love, *Suffering Love*, now grown to manhood, moves in steady stride and humble mien among men who are troubled and doubtful, looking for the "consolation" that seems slow in coming. He goes along the lanes; He enters humble homes; He ministers and feeds and heals, and sometimes, He even raised to life those that were dead. He does more. He admonishes, reproves, rebukes. Men now think Him critical and harsh, and they become vengeful. They lose interest in Him and concern for His welfare. He sometimes complains that He has not where to lay His weary head.

SCENE 3—Suffering Love moves by geometrical progression into its higher forms, and we have *Forgiving Love.* The Hero is arrested by the edicts of the law. He is delivered by a puppet ruler, judged by a biased jury, and finally executed by hired mercenaries. The scene is hastened. The spleen of the court and the hatred of the populace are all too evident. When the evil designs are in the act of fulfillment, He cries out "Father, forgive them, for they know not what they do."

SCENE 4—*Conquering Love* is the last and final of all love. Suffering Love lay buried but it could not be holden. Love comes forth from His narrow bed and prepares to return to the old homestead where He promised to make ready for all who come in their own time. The scene ends with a beautiful tableau, when from a little hill He takes His flight as the company of loved ones look on, some in fear and trembling, and others with unspeakable joy.

Truly that was a great love. "Greater love hath no man than this that he lay down his life for his friends." Could it be that the love was too great? Does the end justify the means? As we look back 1900 years, we wonder did God make a mistake? Did He pay too much? Men are even yet engulfed in jealousies. They are quarreling over mammon, and are ready to destroy without mercy if they can but attain their desired end. Yet we are reminded that a single soul is worth saving, for it is written, "There is joy among the angels in heaven over one sinner that repenteth."

Having observed in roughly sketched outline, what love has done, we may with propriety come to *Love's Demands*. God still loves and God still expects our answer. John spoke for himself and for all who are faithful. It is the chosen few who are able to say from the heart, "He loved us and so we are going to love Him."

In suffering love we observed that God's love was a very humble love. "He humbled Himself and became obedient even unto death." If love stood alone, it would not be so difficult to sign on the dotted line. Going before this great responsive love, there is something which we have sometimes forgotten. "If we confess our sins, He is faithful and just to forgive us our sins and to cleanse us from all unrighteousness." Some deny the very existence of sin, and it may be for the purpose of avoiding confession.

If man is fearfully and wonderfully made, he is most wonderful in dodging responsibility. He would rather take home to his wife a nosegay of the choicest rosebuds than to acknowledge his meanness; and ihs wife is heard to say, "Isn't John the sweetest, dearest ever? He always was that way." With God it is different. He still insists, "Sign on the dotted line."

It is not sufficient to remove from the heart the native or acquired evil. There must be a defi-

nite giving of such as we have for value received.
Silver and gold we do not have. Appreciation, a
mere thank you, may be as unworthy as it is
sometimes formal. Paul enumerates a long list
of gifts such as the heart of man may offer to
Him who loved so valiantly and with such great
efficacy. There is the praise of the lips; the giving of the hand in service; or the bestowal of
goods to feed the poor, but none of these is of
any avail if it stands alone. "Sign on the dotted
line," says the Master. "I want the love of the
heart."

Love is needed at every angle of life; love to
our Christian brother; love to our neighbor, love
to our enemy; all these are required but most of
all there is love toward Him who first loved us.
Love flows from the heart of God. It is stored in
the chambers of the heart for ready and daily use.
Only the heart which is filled can furnish the
needed supply. The empty heart is only a danger
signal.

You know the story of the empty house and its
wicked occupant. The house became most dangerous when it was vacant. The evil spirit grew
tired of the neglected old house. He wanted fresh
air and out he went to seek it. In the meantime
the housekeeper got busy and cleaned the house,
and varnished the floors, and put new runners
on the tables and changed the furniture around.
The evil spirit sauntered by, perhaps out of pure
curiosity, and when he saw how fine it was, he
went out and brought his friends and there were

eight of them in the house. The housekeeper made the mistake of not getting a new tenant at once. Like the empty house, so is the empty heart. Nature abhorring a vacuum, uses little discretion in filling the vacancy. Keep the heart filled. Since it is love that must flow from it, keep it filled with love.

The problem is how to keep the heart filled. There is a way. A friend of mine complained that the battery of his car was run down. It was empty. Later he discovered that the trouble was with the generator. There is a generator for the human heart. The charging element for the human heart is the electric impulse that flows from the great heart of God. That impulse operates through the Word, as it is taught or preached, but the wonder of wonders is that there are still to be found so-called children of God who think that the heart can be charged for a whole year by the electric spasm of a few Lenten services and one communion at Easter.

> "For the love of God is broader
> 　Than the measure of the mind;
> And the heart of the Eternal
> 　Is most wonderfully kind.
>
> "If our love were but more simple
> 　We should take Him at His word;
> And our lives would be all sunshine
> 　In the sweetness of His word."

Jesus and the Cross

OSCAR F. BLACKWELDER

JESUS AND THE CROSS

I. If I Could Be Like Him

DUST storms and floods! These natural catastrophes of recent years illustrate the futility of a self-centered way of life. Following the war, many farmers were not content to market cattle from their grasslands. They insisted on plowing up the grass to plant crops they thought would be more profitable without thought of national welfare. Removal of grass prepared the way for the disastrous dust storms. And the lack of adequate governmental protection for our forests enabled ruthless commercial interests to butcher the woodlands of America. Trees consume millions of gallons of water and handle it safely. The removal of forests and the destruction of grasslands greatly increased the devastating power of floods. These national experiences illustrate this basic fact—the person who takes out of the earth, out of his associates, out of humanity more than he puts in is helping to make life a desert. He is helping to cause the social dust storms, such as sit-down strikes and depressions. He is turning loose upon society the flood miseries of unemployment, partisanship and war.

Many men today confess they have lost their

157

way. A prominent American teacher has written, "The chief characteristic of the present age is its despair of any constructive philosiphy. The result is disillusionment." The answer to this despair and misunderstanding is the cross of Christ. Our attitude toward that cross is an index of our direction in life. Too many men live by a watch instead of a compass. They have a fleeting sense of time but no sure consciousness of direction or guidance. A watch must be changed or set as often as one crosses a time zone, but the compass is good around the world. Many people change ideals and lose their way as often as they cross a social time zone. A compass is good in every social setting. The cross of Christ is to the spiritual world what the compass is in the physical world of sense and sight.

Some years ago on a great American's birthday a metropolitan newspaper carried the picture of a ten-year-old boy with his cap in his hands, gazing at the picture on the wall before him of this remarkable man. The small boy was portrayed as saying: "Oh, if I could be like him!" Today as we reflect on the magnetic personality of the Christ, we say as did this lad: "Oh, if I could be like Him!"

Jesus had the true sense of direction. On the "Mount of Temptation" He said, "Get thee behind me." He could say this because He knew what was in front of Him. The cross of Jesus is the sign of the direction in which His whole life was supremely going. That powerful hymn, "Onward, Christian Soldiers," emphasizes this truth in the line, "With the cross of Jesus going on before." If we are to be like Him we must find our direction in the dynamic experience of His cross. There God's will can be made clear to us. There we can find the power to heal our yesterdays, to overcome the sins of today and to find guidance for tomorrow.

Not only does the cross reveal Christ's sense of *direction* but it also shows His sense of *appreciation*. One of our beautiful Christmas paintings is Lerolle's "The Arrival of the Shepherds." In this painting the shepherds stand huddled together against the rough timbers that support the roof of the stable. One shepherd lifts his hand in allegiance. A second has dropped on his knees in adoration. The third shepherd is a young man who, standing on tiptoe, gazes into the lighted face of the Infant, nestled on His mother's breast, and seeks to find in that lighted face the answer to the riddle of life. Profound as is the incarnation of Christ, the cross holds another secret of life. Not only is Christ *in* us, which is the meaning of the Incarnation, but He is also *for* us, which is the true significance of the cross. By His death on the cross Jesus said forever that man is worth dying for. The cross is Christ's answer to those who take a low view of human worth and destiny. The real meaning of humanity is writ large on the cross and the way is there provided by which men can enter that quality of life with which disease, death, and poverty have nothing to do. The cross is the key to Christ, Christ is the key to God, and God is the source of life. Nothing enables a man to appreciate the meaning of life as does the cross.

Moreover the cross reveals Christ's sense of *obligation*. This cross is often presented as a minus sign. It is too frequently interpreted to mean what we give up. Giving up something dearly prized is deeply inherent in the cross, but the test of life is not primarily what one gives up, but what our giving up enables us to take on. And the cross of Christ is not a division sign. There are those who have construed it to mean mutuality, doing good especially to those of the household of faith, dividing with those who share with us. However, the meaning of the cross is not mutuality but sacrifice. The cross of Christ has been made by some to indicate a multiplication sign and such thinking has inspired the belief that prosperity in one's individual life is the proof of God's blessing. In reality, Christ's cross is a plus sign. "Seek ye first the kingdom of God"—keep the spirit and way of the cross first in life—and all else meaningful shall be *added*.

Jesus erects His cross beside our lives and asks of every one who there has "seen the light" and "felt the burden of his sins rolled away," "What do ye more than others?" May it add to our lives the sense of direction, appreciation and obligation.

II. The Mystery of the Cross

IF the cross were only the story of a man hanging on crossed beams of wood, any good newspaper reporter could tell that in a few paragraphs. After all, it was not hard to tell about the deaths of the two thieves on either side of Christ. But the finest of Christian scholarship, the best of Christian experience, the truest of Christian insight for twenty centuries have not fathomed fully the meaning of the cross. We know too little about men and God to comprehend completely this supreme event of all history.

Consider what the Apostles' Creed, the most widely used creed of Christendom, ventures to say about the cross: "Suffered under Pontius Pilate, was crucified, dead and buried." The cross is infinitely more than that. Great students have gathered their thoughts and Scriptural studies of the years into five outstanding theories about the cross and what it means.

There is the *Ransom theory*. Jesus gave His life a ransom for many. Theologians debated to whom the ransom was paid, but the practical religious consideration is: No matter who received the ransom, are we free men? Have we found the way of release from sin and moral bondage at the foot of the cross? Have we found there the power to conquer evil in our lives?

There is the *Government theory*, which is quite difficult to understand. This much at least seems practical: God was faced with the problem of the government of the world into which evil had come, as sand in the machinery. He sent His Son to handle the problem of evil and through that handling to govern the world from the cross. True Christianity becomes the control of life by the Spirit of Jesus.

There is the *Moral Influence theory*, which speaks in terms like these: Look what love will do, see the lengths to which Jesus went for those He loved and for what He believed. At no place in the long weary road of history have men found such a source of sacrificial living as in the cross. The cross keeps on asking the question: Where were you in 1939 when the world was filled with crucifixion causes?

There is the *Substitutionary theory*, which, said in the language of common folks, reads, He died for me. Here is how sin can be removed from my life and the way opened for fellowship with God. The everyday question lingers on, Is God satisfied with my life? Am I on family terms with God?

And there is the *Reconciliation theory* for "God was in Christ reconciling the world unto Himself." This is the magnetism of the cross—He was lifted up and He is drawing men unto Himself. He is wooing men back to the heart of God. He is the "power of God unto salvation."

Whichever one, or more, of these five conceptions of the cross you accept, and there is great truth in every one, the point of this presentation

is that the cross is still more than a combination
of them all. All of our conceptions and definitions
are like an effort to wrap a very large package
with too small a piece of wrapping paper. Say
the best word you can about the cross, say all you
can, say the last word, and the cross is more than
that, for "all the light of sacred story gathers
round its head sublime." There is a mystery about
the cross which belongs to its deepest meaning.

And, further, the cross of mystery is at home
in a world of mystery. Earth's highest beauty
beauty is born in the womb of tragic mystery.
There is no greater mystery than that of suffering. The world is filled with crosses, and unless
there is a greater cross by which to interpret,
handle, save or heal our crosses, there is no real
or constructive meaning to life. The divine tragedy is at home in a world of tragedy.

I have a friend who went out on his front porch
early one winter morning when his family was
away from home, and he was very lonely. Nature
seemed to be asleep, covered with a blanket of
snow. The universe appeared indifferent, but a
little bird came out to sing and the loneliness of
my friend's heart was answered through that
bird's song. It seemed to say that something was
alive, that love was there, and that the heart of
the universe was friendly. A modern astronomer
asked that these words be inscribed upon his
tomb: "I have loved the stars too fondly to be
fearful of the night." Who taught that bird to
sing? Who lit that friendly star? I believe it was

the same, heart, mind, life, and God who speaks
through the cross. A song, a star, a cross—and
the greatest of these is a cross. That "scaffold
holds the future." "Behind the dim unknown
standeth God within the shadows, keeping watch
above His own." There is a mystery about the
cross which has made it the only cross, though
crosses are scattered all along the path of history.
Yes, there were three crosses on Calvary, but the
one in the middle was different—"it was lumi-
nous with God." The mystery of the cross is at
home in a world of mystery.

And, still further, the only way to interpret
the mystery of the cross is through the mystery
of personality. We believe in the cross because
we believe in Jesus. It is more like Him than
anything else He ever did. There is more of Him
in it. He was the only One who understood what
was going on that day. His last seven words have
been called windows through which to study what
was passing in His mind. His last seven senten-
ces are His explanation of the purpose of His own
death. We believe in the cross because we believe
in Jesus.

The mystery of the cross can be studied in
what it does to human personality across the
centuries. Look what it has done with people.
Faltering sinners have smitten their breasts and
cried, "God be merciful to me a sinner." "Many
a son of the mountains has knelt there dreaming"
—"forgetting the things which are behind and
reaching forth to those things which are before."

The cross is life's eternal plus. What a man is now plus Jesus equals the man he ought to be. The finer a person one becomes, the less conscious he is of his achievements in personal character or social accomplishment and honestly confesses, "Nothing in my hands I bring, simply to Thy cross I cling."

III. JESUS, THE CHURCH AND AMERICA

TWO things are wrong with the world: evil and stupidity. It is the task of the church not only to face the problem of evil with the redemption of Christ but to contribute consecrated intelligence toward the solution of the problem of stupidity.

First, the church ought to be the spear point in the struggle for human freedom. We hear much today, and we will likely hear more tomorrow about freedom of speech, freedom of the press, and freedom of worship. The first two are safeguarded by the third. When freedom of worship goes, the final bulwark of freedom is gone.

What is the real meaning of equality about which the Declaration of Independence speaks? Not social equality, nor physical or intellectual equality! Not even equality before the law—for that is a derived equality. What is the implication of oaths in a court house? Why not take an oath to the court or to the judge if the law is ultimate in itself?

The only equality in this world is equality before God. In a certain Washington church a Chinese laundryman, a scrub woman and a cabinet member joined the congregation the same morning. In welcoming them the pastor said, "The floor gets level at the foot of the cross." Where else does it get level? The only democracy in this world is the universal priesthood of believers. The church must so guard and use freedom of worship, calling men and women through penitence and forgiveness to enter this priesthood and bringing social problems that crush human lives under the searching light of Jesus, that such religious debacles as Russia and Germany may not be reproduced here. Thus the church can be the spear point in the struggle for freedom.

Second, the church should lay those moral foundations upon which a finer economic order can be erected. Our widespread inability to think morally as well as technically on economic problems increases the difficulty of our days. Even some religious folks, instead of contributing such spiritual and moral insight as they may possess, are talking about the end of the world and the second coming of Christ. It is easy to fold one's hands, relax one's mind, and wait for Him. That can be moral cowardice of the worst type—as if He were not here now, as if the Incarnation, Crucifixion and Resurrection were untrue, as if these historic experiences did not mean His Presence today. It is the task of the church to interpret and present the living Churst so as to undergird the whole structure of man's personal and social life.

The practical question which reveals the difference between current economic theories is: what is the purpose of life? Upon the answer to that question hangs all economic thinking. Communism has its answer, as do Fascism and Naziism. Evangelical Christians can not accept those answers. Someone has said that the first business of the preacher is to tell people what they are.

If man is made in the image of God for the ultimate purpose of achieving sonship with God, then man is a spiritual personality, not cannon fodder for dictators, not a unit of a totalitarian state, not the pawn of an economic collectivism. This world is not intended primarily to be a machine, dedicated to efficiency, but a home, dedicated to brotherhood. In thus insisting upon man's essential character, being and destiny, the church can lay the moral foundation upon which alone a finer economic order may be built.

Third, the church must show the relation between religion and democracy. One of my friends suggests a word of five letters to describe the world today. That word is "split." The world is split vertically into nations; nations are split horizontally into races; races are split obliquely into classes; within classes homes are split as the increasing divorce rate indicates; within homes are what the psychologists call split personalities. We have been leaving out a kind of cement necessary to hold life together. What is that "cement"?

I suggest religion. The very word religion means a "bond" or "tie," uniting a man to God, to his fellow men everywhere and an inward tie becoming his "integrating principle," uniting and sustaining his life and preventing a split personality. Such religion is not simply a principle, a thesis, a set of rules, abstract righteousness, or social tradition. At its best religion means Jesus Christ. He is man's "tie" and "bond." Jesus alone can be the "cement" adequate to hold men together and make possible the very existence of society.

There are at least four ways to face human differences. They can be fought out—that is the military way; they can be argued out—that is the business way; they can be compromised—that is the political way; they may be transcended—that is the Christian way. Christ is the only loyalty greater than race, nation, or tradition. He alone can insure the solidarity and the very existence of the social order.

Fourth, the church should keep the mind of Christ in general circulation so that man's sense of justice may be sharp and dependable.

An American newspaper recently said that the only appeal greater than to the United States Supreme Court is the appeal to the future. But there is a higher appeal than that—the appeal to the past, present and future, which is the ultimate. And that is God.

The practical expression of justice for the average man is known as the Golden Rule, "Do unto

others as you would have them do unto you." Few
influences have confused men's minds more than
that statement. Certainly Jesus taught it, but to
His disciples who had made the commitment of
their lives to Him and thus had the way opened
by which they could live on the higher reaches
of life rather than the average or the lower.

This rule can be most selfishly applied. It is
easily conceivable for persons in comfortable
economic circumstances to become cold and indifferent, for they do not want much back from
other men, and so they give little of themselves
to men. The Golden Rule puts a man and his own
wishes at the center of his life. He himself becomes the yardstick and measurement of all he
wants and gives. And this rule can be practiced
on all levels in life, even by dope fiends and
gangsters.

Principles are higher than rules, so I preach to
you "The Diamond Principle." No dope fiend can
practice that. It takes man out of the center of
his thinking and provides a higher measurement
than his own judgment of what is right and
wrong. This Diamond Principle reads: Do unto
others as Jesus would have you do unto them.

A man who is only just will soon be less than
just. Justice does not have the power to keep
itself sharpened. The big question is, Who knows
what is just? It takes love and God to keep justice alive in men's minds and lives. Love and
God meet in Jesus and climax in His cross. There
is, therefore, only one real need in the world—

justice through Jesus. His presence in men's minds will keep their sense of justice sharp and dependable.

I never believed in Jesus Christ for as many reasons as I do today. It is literally Christ or chaos. What is your Lenten answer?

IV. THE EYES OF THE SOUL

THE soul has eyes, or how could Helen Keller see? Fading physical sight and increasing inner light wrote, "O Love that wilt not let me go." A blind Milton saw a "Paradise Regained." A sightless Fanny Crosby desired the passing "Gentle Saviour."

When love is done, life goes blind. Love can be analyzed into the true, the beautiful, the good. When these three are discovered in love, life has found its final philosophy, and the soul will not go blind. When they are separated, love degenerates into sentiment, and then arises the greatest moral problem of our generation: enjoyment without obligation. The true, the beautiful, the good are united classically in the thirteenth chapter of First Corinthians, the love lyric of the New Testament.

Suffering may send the soul blind, but "love suffers long." Suffering and music are universal languages. To study the meaning of suffering is to listen to the deeper chords of life. Who best can suffer best can do. Great poetry is often the

story of broken dreams. Elizabeth Browning is
not alone in turning a bed of affliction into a
mount of transfiguration. The perfect picture of
Jesus is as the Suffering Servant.

Yet for many, suffering is the sweat of the soul,
and salty water burns the eyes and blinds. Love
can keep the soul from going blind through suffering for "love beareth all things." Hate is like
a brittle reed; love is like an oak tree. Love is
the strongest thing in the world. Love keeps the
heart fires burning. Life's only enduring interpretation is love. All things work together for
good to those that love God. Love is life's perfect
tense, for love suffers long.

Envy may send the soul blind, but "love envies
not." Envy paralyzes pure motives and shuts out
the fresh air. It turns the bright cloud dark side
out. It reduces enthusiasm to criticism. It writes
no songs, builds no cathedrals. It makes the user
do his worst in the presence of the best. It speaks
behind hand-covered mouths. It makes cowards.
It is the password to the fraternity of the defeat-
ed. It makes others beside Judas use a handshake
as the symbol of friendship and a kiss as the
symbol of love to betray true friends. Envy blunts
the point and dulls the edge of life. It makes
judgments inacurate. If life be a foot-race, envy
is stiff-arming the one who runs next to you; both
are slowed up, the goal is no nearer, either may
lose his balance.

Love alone can keep the soul from going blind
through envy, for "love believeth all things."

Love believes in the right of every man to run his race. Love believes in the birthright of every life to come to its own highest development. Love believes in every man's chance to prophesy according to his own proportion of faith. The Great Scorer will not ask "Did you win or lose?" but "How did you play the game?" "To live above low hatreds and revenges, cultivate the habit of looking behind men to God." Love envies not.

Pride may send the soul blind, but "love vaunteth not itself, is not puffed up, doth not behave itself unseemly, seeketh not her own." Life is largely a matter of angles, the way we look at situations and people. These angles are now called attitudes. How different the view from a high mountain or tall building, and how foolish to climb these high places with a weak heart. Pride is like that.

One of America's greatest teachers of English literature recently died, and at the close of the funeral service, by his request, a colored quartet sang, "Swing Low, Sweet Chariot, Coming for to Carry Me Home." America thought him at the top of the ladder. His own estimate was that the chariot of the Lord would have to come down low to find him. A Scotch preacher lay ill in his home. A neighbor called and whispered in his ear, "Safe in the arms of Jesus." Rallying his fading strength, the Scotchman answered, "No, at His feet." Love is like that.

Pride is revealed in whether, and what, we worship. The problem of America, unlike that of the Orient, is not that we shall have too many gods, but that we shall have no God. Will Rogers is right in judging a man, not by his face, but by getting behind him and seeing what he is looking at. A man lives in his reverences and his reverences measure his pride.

There is no more misunderstood word in our language than sacrifice. It is not something we do when our backs are against the wall. It is rather that which must be done in order really to live. The path of love leads to the place of sacrifice and at that place the flowers of humility grow. No one can be humble who has not sacrificed. The heart of humility is to sacrifice one's will to His.

Love will keep the soul from going blind through pride because "love hopeth all things." Love hopes the most and not the least for all men. Love hopes that the best man will win. Love hopes and hungers for the triumph of truth. Far more than the pride of a man's own opinion is his right to the truth, which alone sets men free. Truth is the language of love. Love is not puffed up and seeketh not her own.

Worry may send the soul blind, but "love is not easily provoked." There is the worry that comes from great responsibility. There is the worry of broken confidences. There is the worry of fading strength and growing cares. But why make worry an added responsibility and care? It is the worm inside the apple. Worry reduces vitality, weakens the power of the mind to judge correctly, impairs the courage of the will. Worry and not work provides the nervous breakdowns. Work may wear out, but worry burns out. It destroys. Many problems can be prayed out that can not be thought out any other way, but no problem was ever worried out. That is not thinking. It is the destruction of the thinking processes. It is killing the hen that lays the golden egg. The foreground of worry is nervousness, and the background is fear.

Adequate religion must deal with this increasing disease of nervousness and fear. It can not alone be the task of the psychiatrist. It requires more than a process of "re-education." Because a man makes a failure of his business does not mean he must make a failure of his life.

Love alone can keep the soul from going blind through worry. For "love endureth all things." Perfect love casteth out fear. Love throws light on the darkness of worry. Love brings patience to the weariness of worry. Love undergirds the discouragements of worry with the courage of faith. Love casts out the sin of worry with its own white purity. Love quiets nerves. Love reunites family firesides. Love is the silver cord that finally brings the wanderer home. Love pours peace on troubled waters. Love endures.

And *evil* may send the soul blind, but "love thinketh no evil, rejoiceth not in iniquity, but rejoiceth in the truth."

Love alone can keep the soul from going blind through evil, for "love never fails." Love makes evil fail. Love works her way into the nooks and crannies of life and becomes the mortar to build the temple of His Spirit. It holds life together. It completes the circle. Love is fellowship with the truth. He that loves will be made perfect. Love can not fail.

"The ideal life is in our blood and never will be still. We feel the thing we ought to be beating beneath the thing we are. Every time we see a man who has attained our ideal more fully than we have, it awakens our languid blood and fills us with new longings." This is the appeal of Jesus. He is what we would like to be and has what we would like to have. In a competitive, calculating, critical world, love is often repeated as a dream, but distrusted as a method. It just will not work. But here is one life that has lived it, and the centuries do Him honor. When Paul's experience is ours, and "Christ liveth in us," He has set our feet on the way of love.

When the tree falls in the forest and no one is present to hear, there is no sound. Sound and love can not be impersonal. Love does not exist as the natural power of gravitation. It is not a principle. Love reveals itself not in books or axioms, but alone in people. The only eternal facts are personal. Jesus is love made real. Jesus is love spelled out in human life. We can be the extension of His personality.

Love is the way to interpret Calvary, where the broken heart of the Saviour is within hand reach of mankind. The cross is love's necessity. Love is the infinite longing to bestow oneself. Him whom the heavens can not contain dwells in the heart that loves. To know the love of Christ which passeth knowledge means to be filled with the fullness of God and to make personal and modern the love lyric of the New Testament. Faith will be changed to sight, hope will end in vision, but love is changeless and eternal.

The Christian Life and the Modern Tempo

E. S. HJORTLAND

THE CHRISTIAN LIFE AND THE MODERN TEMPO

I. THE POISE OF JESUS

IF we could call from the past any one of the twelve disciples and ask him what characteristic of Jesus impressed him the most, I believe he would say the poise of Jesus, His controlled emotional energy always wisely directed. If we leaf through the Gospels and with our imaginnations re-create the scenes and sounds which took place, we, too, will be impressed with the poise of the Saviour.

One evening as the Master with His faithful few approached a Samaritan village, they were warned that their presence was not desired. The disciples becoming very indignant turned to Jesus and said: "Wilt thou that we bid fire to come down from heaven, and consume them?" But Jesus rebuked His own disciples, saying, "Ye know not what manner of spirit ye are of, for the Son of Man came not to destroy men's lives, but to save them."

When Jesus came to visit His home town Nazareth, with which were associated many pleasant boyhood memories, He preached to the people in the local synagogue. The response, however, was

179

not very favorable, and the people in great anger took Him to the edge of the village to plunge Him headlong over the cliff, but "He passing through the midst of them went his way." The multitudes also observed in this man a composure and a manner not found in the religious leaders of that day. When Jesus finished the Sermon on the Mount, they marveled at His sayings, "for he taught them as one having authority, and not as the scribes." And on one occasion soldiers were sent to take Him, but when they found Him, they abandoned their plans and listened attentively, and came away saying: "No man spake like this man!"

The disciples felt that Jesus should temper some of His strong statements. They felt He should compromise at certain points and therefore admonished Him saying: "Wist ye not that the Pharisees were offended in you this day?" But instead of being frightened by this warning, He openly exposed the hypocrisy of the Pharisees.

Look at the Saviour in the Garden of Gethsemane when His enemies came with swords and staves to start Him on the weary road to Calvary! The disciples became very excited. Peter whipped out a sword and struck at one of the soldiers as would a frightened, hysterical person. Jesus restrained him with the words: "Put up thy sword, for they that take to the sword shall perish by the sword." Not long after, the disciples took to their legs and ran from the scene like frightened children.

Turn to your Gospels and follow Jesus from Gethsemane through to the long hours on the cross, and you will become fully aware of the divine composure of the Saviour. See Him as He stands before King Herod! The dissolute king is surrounded by fawning courtiers. There in the tinseled pageantry of the court stands the peasant, Jesus of Nazareth. With "many words" Herod questions Him, and very likely boastfully displays his views on the philosophy of religion and life. Here is an opportunity for Jesus to play up to the vanity of Herod and by a few words of flattery obtain His freedom, but to the surprise of all present, and Herod included, Jesus remains completely silent! He answered Herod not a word. What would we have done in a similar situation?

And when Jesus stands before Pilate, who has dealt with kings and statesmen and criminals, and begins the trial of this troublesome Jew in a perfunctory manner, it is not long before it becomes the trial of Pilate before Jesus! The steady gaze of this fearless man who stands before him, his freedom from all wild pleading to spare His life, is very disconcerting to King Pilate. "I find no fault in this man," he says, and tries in various ways to escape passing judgment upon Him. As the trial moves along, Pilate becomes more confused and troubled, and in the end he loses his poise and turns Jesus over to the whims of the mob and the hate-filled priests.

Or there is Jesus hanging on the cross, His

body wracked with pain. Before Him are the tormentors crying out: "Come down from the cross! If thou be the Son of God, save thyself!" "He saved others; himself he can not save," they sneer. And yet Jesus could say to this group: "Father, forgive them, for they know not what they do!" What would we have said if we had been in His place? The centurion who had charge of the crucifixion of Jesus, and who had no doubt gone through this gruesome task many times before, felt himself gripped by what he saw and heard, and said loud enough for others to hear: "Surely this was a righteous man! Surely he was the Son of God!"

The poise of Jesus becomes more and more apparent to us when our own experience in this world becomes extensive and we meet in a small way with the same temptations and trials which were heaped upon Jesus. But how do *we* act? Do we keep our poise?

When the Titanic went down, a partially loaded lifeboat was pushing away from the sinking hull when a man swam up to one end of the lifeboat and sought to climb in. A woman took an oar and furiously beat his hands until he let go. He floated down toward the other end of the boat and someone reached over, pulled him in and saved his life. If you had been in that boat, how would you have acted? Like the first or second person?

It is very easy for us, sitting at home in a comfortable chair, to state how we would act in a given situation, but it is quite another thing to make a wise decision in the midst of excitement, fear, darkness, and impending death. It requires no great amount of intelligence or courage to sit in the grandstand and call the signals for the team out on the field. It is vastly different to remain calm when we see the minutes slipping by and know that an unwise decision, or a workable play too hastily or too slowly executed, may cost the game. Not a few of the critics of the government, of the church, and of the schools, are grandstand players. Their composed pulling apart of our institutions and established moral standards is done in the quiet of a private study.

How do we act when wealth suddenly falls into our lap? Do we suddenly put on airs, forget our former friends, and treat roughly those who have not as much of this world's goods as we have? Do we keep our poise as did George Peabody, who quietly went about spending his possessions to alleviate the suffering of mankind, and yet did it without a patronizing air and without losing faith in his fellow men?

Or how about the experience of poverty? If tomorrow you were to lose your job, your source of income were to be taken from you, would you become bitter and reproachful toward your fellow men, blame the government, blame industry? Would you sink into a mood of bitterness and reproach which would be felt by your wife and children and friends? Or would you make poverty your schoolmaster to develop in your character the ability to see values which you had heretofore missed? Would you discover the meaning of friendship, the joy of good health, of eyesight? A beggar once complained that he did not have shoes; then he saw another beggar who had no feet, and he ceased to complain.

Can you keep your poise? If suddenly you were to be steeped in great sorrow, as some of you may have experienced quite recently; if something or someone closely bound with your happiness were suddenly removed from your life, would you keep your poise? Or would you draw shades over the windows of your soul and there by yourself keep dreaming about yesterday, about what might have been, continually sifting through your hands the ashes of yesterday's broken castles? Or would you take your affliction and use it to sweeten the melody of your life's song? Harry Lauder, when his son was killed in the World War, said he had the choice of drowning his sorrow in drink or putting himself into his singing with greater intensity and greater earnestness. The stirring music which thrilled thousands of soldiers received much of its beauty from the pain in his heart.

Do you keep your poise when the little irritations of life, the criticisms, fall upon your ears? Do you give way to the temptations to be jealous, to be sarcastic, to put someone in his or her place? Do you lose your poise and follow the suggestions of the Old Adam within you? Have you ever come home at night and rehearsed the day's events and severely reproached yourself for some

of the things you have said, wondering why you
acted the way you did, why you kept silent when
you should have spoken, or been harsh when gentle words would have accomplished more good?

Why do we lose our poise? We lose our poise
when it appears that that which we treasure most
is going to be taken from us. Therefore, if a person becomes attached to that which moth and rust
can destroy; if he worships that which is not permanent, he will lose his poise. Jesus kept His
composure because His life was one with that of
God. "I and the Father are one," He said. "I
came not to do my own will, but the will of him
who sent me." Jesus was not attached to anything that could be permanently destroyed.

If a person worships money, honor, or some
person, he will find many times that he will be
losing his poise, because these things can be taken
from him.

Briefly, then, the way to gain poise is by deep-
ening our trust in and our love of God. A Christian has poise because he puts his trust in the
unchanging Jesus Christ, who is the same yesterday, today, and forever. Whatever we as Christians pass through, whether it be sorrow, wealth,
poverty, or the temptation to live life on a low
level, we will find that we can keep our poise
when we worship Him who said: "Be not afraid,
I have oversome the world." And again Jesus
said: "Let not your heart be troubled. My peace
I give unto you. Not as the world giveth, give I
unto you." If you are nervous, distraught, and

upset, and if you are looking for someone to "minister unto a mind diseased," as did Macbeth, I recommend to you the simple pratice of prayer, of getting fixed in your mind that God the Father cares for you and that in Him there is no fear, for "perfect love casteth out fear."

Listen to this seventy-six-year-old woman, the mother of Goethe: "I rejoice in my life because the lamp still glows. I seek by thorny ways; I love the small pleasures of life. If doors are too low I bend; if I can remove a stone from the path, I do so; if it is too heavy, I go around it, and so I find something in every day that pleases me. And the cornerstone, my belief in God, makes my heart glad and my face shining."

II. "THEY FORGOT TO TAKE BREAD"

Mark 8. 14

TODAY we find Jesus and His faithful few sailing across the Sea of Galilee for the village of Bethsaida. Mealtime has arrived, hunger has set in, and they make the disappointing discovery that they have insufficient food, for "they forgot to take bread." All they can discover in their midst is a single loaf, hardly enough to satisfy their outdoor appetites. This act of forgetfulness reveals a weakness not only in the disciples, but one that is common to all of us. To appreciate this incident fully, we must look into the event that preceded their boat trip.

A multitude had gathered in a desert place to listen to the gracious words that fell from the lips of the Master. The hour became late and the people hungry, and the records tell us that Jesus provided them with food. Shortly after this, they went by boat to Bethsaida. The problem of providing bread was completely forgotten by the disciples. Consciously or unconsciously, they omitted to take the necessary food with them. Perhaps they thought Jesus would henceforth provide in a miraculous way all their material needs, that He would meet any emergency that would arise by using His divine power. But we have no record to show that He gave His own disciples bread in a miraculous manner. Very likely He let them go hungry in order to teach them this important lesson: Trust in God does not mean to abandon the use of one's intellect in planning for and meeting the future. Trust in God is not to shut one's eyes and blindly walk forward believing that God will brush away every obstacle and magically provide in all emergencies. This is a truth that we as Christians must keep before us: Our social, moral, and educational problems are not going to be solved by resting on the oars and chanting, "God will take care of us."

There is a tendency on the part of all of us to rely for the solution of all our ills on people and forces outside of ourselves. The present-day doctor is trying to get us away from the idea that as soon as we become ill we should rush to the medicine chest. In quite a few homes the bathroom shelves are lined with a great variety of good and bad medicines which people look to as to magic. Many consider medicine as something that can make up for the absence of self-discipline and wise health-care. The modern doctor thinks more of preventive methods than of cures, bromides, sedatives, and pain removers.

Remember the early pioneers of our country who met every hardship, who lived in poorly-ventilated and unevenly-heated cabins, who faced the dangers of the frontier, the threat of Indians, lawless whites, and wild animals, and yet were alert, strong, and rugged. But we moderns have coddled ourselves, lowered our vitality, and are less alert, because we rely upon outside forces to solve our difficulties. With all our present-day conveniences, we have become a physically and spiritually sleepy people.

Is it not also true that we are waiting for others to entertain us? We crowd around the radio to listen rather than around the piano to sing. We read much, but we do not meditate often or long. We are bored with our own companionship. We become incapable of entertaining ourselves. As soon as something is done for us which we could do ourselves, we are weakened in that direction. There you have one of the drawbacks of giving relief to the unemployed. The morale of many is lowered, and not a few become shiftless and careless; the drive goes out of them; they become passive, dependent creatures because bread is provided for them. Or consider the child who from infancy to maturity is sheltered and spoon-fed. Such a pampered child will crumble like a toy boat in a storm when he ventures out by himself into the real world.

It is always difficult to know where to draw the line in helping another, but we ourselves should make every effort to "work out our own salvation with fear and trembling," and avoid having others do for us what we could do ourselves. God has given us a mind and resources to be used. Hard thinking and careful planning does not show lack of faith; it is the wise use of the gifts that God has given us. Do not justify careless thinking, lack of purpose, and the unwillingness to practice self-discipline by speaking of it as trust in God. If you "forget to take bread" and fail to conform to the rules of life, you will go hungry; you will suffer.

There is an immediate application of this text. We are passing through the Lenten season, and soon we shall come to that great day in the Christian calendar, Easter. Throughout Lent we are having strong emotional experiences. We are walking upon the mountain tops; we are hearing sermons over the radio, from the pulpit, and reading them in our papers. On a mighty tide we are being lifted and carried forward. Many of us are resting upon the oars, and when the Lenten period is over, we will slip back into our old ways and habits and "forget to take bread."

Let us then during this Lenten season resolve to consecrate to God the brains He has given us to plan for the future as He gives us wisdom to see the future, and rigidly hold ourselves to the outline which we believe to be in conformity to His will and for our best. Do not expect God to do for you what you ought to do yourself. Prayer is not an escape; it is not a time when we speak great words of praise and parade our humility before God. We need to stand upon our feet, roll up our sleeves, and face whatever unpleasant tasks lie before us.

This thought should help us in a measure to understand why many of the afflictions and sufferings come to mankind. In former years many lives were lost at sea. Poorly constructed ships, inadequate equipment, and slow travel caused many a disaster. By trial and error, loss of life, numerous experiments, and constant research, ocean travel is today as safe as travel on land. Today a major catastrophe on the ocean is almost a matter of the past. It is as we have blundered and suffered that we have discovered our mistakes, corrected them, and moved on. It is also true in the field of medicine and surgery. We have conquered disease by laborious effort, pains, and relentless application of mind and body. It is not by magic that God has revealed the way of the world to us, but as man has applied his brain and put himself to the problems before him, God has unlocked the mysteries of health and happiness.

To me the miracle of the feeding of the five thousand is not a justification for a relaxed indifference to the demands of tomorrow, but a revelation of the fact that God has abundantly supplied this world with all that we need for this body and life; that here on this earth is enough food for all people; there is no need for starvation. It is by wise use of what we already have, by social planning, and by constant application that we shall solve our economic difficulties. What is lacking upon this earth is not might nor brain capacity, but the *will* to move in the direction of righteousness. For this we must all unite in prayer. We must pray as individuals that God will plant in our hearts a courageous faith, that He will lead us along dangerous paths, over difficult highways, knowing that when we go as far as we can with the gifts we possess, He will not fail us.

Do not use your religion as an escape from reality; but as Christians, confidently move forward, knowing that "all things work together for good to them that love the Lord."

III. "BEHOLD!"

Behold, the Lamb of God, that taketh away the sin of the world! John 1. 29.

THE prophet from the wilderness, John, the forerunner of Jesus, must have been striking in appearance and speech. His raiment was camel's hair and a leathern girdle, and his food was locusts and wild honey. Bluntly, and with little respect for persons, he spoke openly of the sins of his people. In swift, broad strokes he cut away the unctuous piety of certain Pharisees. He exposed their selfishness, their lack of God's grace, and their attempt to conceal it by sweet lip service to religion. John's rugged honesty and vigorous speech made him a man to be avoided by anyone trying to mask a life controlled by low motives. It was to be expected that eventually he would come into conflict with the existing powers.

Every Sunday school book which tells the story of this prophet, John, outlines vividly his fearless exposure of the evil life of the king and queen. John, completely indifferent to consequences, openly attacks King Herod and Queen Herodias. He is cast into prison; Herodias seeks to silence her restless conscience by plotting the death of John. She has him beheaded, and so ends the earthly story of this man whom Jesus singled out and said: "There hath not arisen a greater than John the Baptist."

The greatness of John is not to be found in his nomadic appearance, his simple diet, nor his blunt speech. The secret of his strength is found in the words with which he greets Jesus: "Behold, the Lamb of God, that taketh away the sin of the world," and especially in the one word: "Behold."

The manner in which we approach an idea or an object will in a large measure determine the value it will receive from us. Two people can meet the same experience and yet come out of it with opposite reactions. There are those who in reading the New Testament come away speaking of Jesus as a great moralist, or a superman, and so He was, but to John He was more than a moral Hercules. Some have spoken of Him as a great teacher, and anyone would do well to study the methods of Jesus in directing the thinking of others, but to John, Jesus was the "Lamb of God, that taketh away the sin of the world." He came away with a full evaluation of Jesus because he had formed the habit of a reverent approach to life. Here may be an answer as to why the lives of some people are small and ineffectual, and why they place a low value not alone upon Jesus, but upon all they touch. They lack the reverent approach to life.

What do we mean by reverent approach? First, it is to handle the things of this world with a sense of awe. This feeling can more easily be illustrated than defined. It comes over us when we view a sight like the Grand Canyon, or Niagara Falls, or a snow-covered mountain range. When we have been inspired by the stars of night, have we not found ourselves saying: "The heavens declare the glory of God," and we understand then what the Psalmist meant when he said: "Deep calling unto deep."

Or have you ever fished in the North Woods on a warm summer evening, and watched the sun go down, the darkness settle upon the earth, and a full moon rise above the horizon, lighting the landscape with its silvery rays? When you saw the trees dimly outlined against the sky, a boat moving in the shadows with its oarlocks creaking, a gentle breeze ruffling the water—did you not experience a feeling of awe? Did you not feel that you were in the presence of God? Did not your soul seem to say: "Behold!"?

There are other ways, too, in which the Divine Presence becomes as real to us as the hand of a friend upon the shoulder. Have you ever walked through the nursery in a hospital and looked at those tiny infants and speculated as to their future? Or it may be that you have sat with someone who is slowly letting go of the last threads of his earthly pattern, and you have felt the mystery of life and death coming over you, a sense of awe. Behold! Or it may be that you yourself had a close brush with the angel of death, and then in those days when you were regaining strength, people and scenes passed before your mind, and you rearranged them in an order quite different from the way in which you had heretofore placed them.

A sense of awe in the presence of the divine may come into a person's mind in the reading of a good book, or a thoughtful poem, or perhaps by the touch of a strong personality. For a moment you are lifted out of the usual path of life and you hear the Psalmist say: "Be still and know that I am God."

In the city—and the larger the city the more it is true—the sense of awe easily slips away from us. We are constantly in the midst of explainable things. Street cars, automobiles, buildings, adding machines, typewriters, and radios—though we may not understand or know how to create any of these material things ourselves, yet we do know that there are men who can explain and create these objects with which we are constantly surrounded. We tend, if anything, to admire the nimble wits of man rather than worship the greatness of God. There is good reason why people who live close to the soil suffer less from nervousness than those who live in large cities, for the man upon the farm is not many steps removed from the eternal Creator.

There is another part to reverence which space permits me only to suggest. It is the attitude of high expectancy. A child at Christmas time eagerly tears open his gift packages; his whole attitude is one of high expectancy. The bride and groom, as they dream of the home they are to establish, as they visualize its unfolding, do so in a spirit of expectancy. The feeling is expressed by these lines:

> "I love preliminary things—
> The tuning up of flutes and strings,
> The little scrolls musicians play,
> The varying keys to feel their way,
> The hum—the hush in which it dies,
> But most to see the curtain rise."

But this air of expectancy has gone out of the lives of many. They wearily check off each day from the calendar, going through the motions of living while their souls are dead. I know that there are plausible explanations for this absence of a joyous outlook upon life. The threat of world war, unemployment, economic insecurity, the ceaseless struggle to make ends meet, and personal troubles are present to plague us; and yet, in spite of these things, the Christian must believe with all his heart that "all things work together for good to them that love the Lord." The Christian must have fixed in his mind that the will of God is for our good, and the test of our faith is our steadfast hold on this great truth.

This, then, is what we mean by reverence: a sense of awe and a feeling of high expectancy. Why is this attitude so important? It helps to restrain the ego; we are less likely to rush in where angels fear to tread. "How then can I do this great wickedness, and sin against God?" said Joseph. It also makes us much more alert mentally. We are going to see what the confirmed pessimist discards or overlooks. The man who approaches life with a reverent attitude keeps moving when others are inclined to quit; he will not commit the sin of "putting his hand to the plough and looking backward." Furthermore, it will keep us from forming a low estimate of our fellow men. We will not put property and possessions above human life. When David and Abishai came upon the sleeping Saul, Abishai raised his spear and was ready to kill the king, but David said: "Lay not thy hand upon the Lord's anointed!" The reverent approach to human life is much needed today.

In closing, may I say that if you wish to retain

this reverent approach, move in the presence of the thoughts of great men and women. Join with movements greater than yourself. Draw aside from the crowd, and each day make it a point to meditate upon God's Word, and wait until His spirit and power descend upon you. "They that wait upon the Lord shall renew their strength."

IV. A Misplaced Halo

NOT every village, not every home welcomed a visit from Jesus, the Galilean carpenter. A Samaritan hamlet refused Him entrance, much to the indignation of the disciples with Him. Even in Nazareth, a place bound up with His boyhood days, the people sought by force to get Him out of the town. There were other towns, both large and small, that joyfully waited for His coming. There were honest homes of both rich and poor whose doors were opened wide at the sound of His approaching footsteps. Such was the village of Bethany, and such was the home of Mary and Martha and Lazarus. By walking leisurely one could reach Bethany from the thriving metropolitan center, Jerusalem, in about an hour's time. To this cluster of peaceful homes nestled in a hillside Jesus often resorted.

Those days preceding His trial, His brutal treatment, unfair handling by secular and religious authorities, He quietly slipped off to this slumbering village to fix more firmly His convic-

tion "that he must go up to Jerusalem to suffer
many things at the hands of the chief priests and
the elders, and at last be put to death."

It is here that we find Jesus in today's meditation. While here, a strange display of devotion
was enacted. Strange to the disciples who witnessed it, and doubly strange to us at this distance
in time and understanding from the actual scene.
Mary, who it is generally believed had suffered
from some malady classed as possession of seven
demons, came into the room with a cruse of costly
ointment and proceeded to pour it on Jesus, both
on His head and feet, and then she wiped His feet
with her hair. It helps us somewhat to know that
oil was frequently used in this manner to protect
the skin from the summer heat, that perfume was
also handled like money. One stored it and drew
upon it as we would a bank account in order to
obtain other desired articles.

The disciples frowned disapprovingly on the
whole drama. "Why this waste?" they whispered,
and perhaps added: "Just like an impractical
woman!" Jesus not only failed to condemn the
woman, He praised her, for He saw what the
others did not see. It was an act of devotion, of
gratitude, for Mary had not tried to do and give
as little as possible and get by with it, but her
heart urged her to be generous, and to give her
best.

Now we could spend our time on just that
thought. How the manner in which we worship
God reflects the measure of our sincerity. "Where

a man's treasure is, there will his heart be also";
and where a man's heart is, you will also find his
purse, his enthusiasm, his thoughts, his whole
being. True devotion seeks to express itself in
beauty, and is not content until it does so.

But it is this man Judas who engages our attention today—the man who acted as treasurer of
the faithful few, he who held the bag. As he saw
the oil being poured upon the feet and head of
Jesus, and on the floor, he saw not oil but silver
coins slipping between his fingers. Graciously he
conceals his feelings and seizes the occasion to
slip a halo upon his own head. "This," he said
weightily and solemnly, "should have been sold
and the money given to the poor." His money-
measuring mind quickly estimates its worth: "It
could have been sold for three hundred shillings."

The approach that Judas made to the generous
gesture of devotion on the part of Mary is not un-
common. We get into the habit of measuring all
that we contact with a rod of dollars and cents.
We measure a job by how much it pays; we measure people by their incomes. Here is someone we
have ignored, and then one day we learn that he
has money, and we suddenly brighten up, and our
manners improve. We move from one city to another, we pick our associates by whether they add
to our purse or not. Carnegie and Frank Doubleday, when playing golf, compared their occupa-
tions. When Carnegie found that Doubleday was
not making a huge profit, he said: "Get out of it

and get into something else where there is more money!"

When we make money our gauge for measuring people and things, we shut the door to other values. Such a person will never know the value of the smile of a child, the commendation of a kindly and wise elderly person, the security of a happy home, the joy of being sought by good people, the happiness of being trusted, the warm glow that comes when one has joined with others in creating something permanently good. Such a person shuts for himself the door to music, a symphony can not break through the wooden walls of his heart and bring out the high and low moods and all the various shades of thought of which the human mind is capable. He hears no song of the morning songbirds, for he is on his way to the market place; he fails to see the setting sun like a huge bonfire at the road's end, for he is reckoning the day's wages.

Such a man knows nothing about the heartache of his neighbors, the big tears of the child who sits before his broken toys, the ambition in the young man to strike out against the mountain and the sea, nor the wistful dreams of the maiden to establish her own home. He knows nothing of the fierce struggle against despair by someone beaten and twisted by ruthless hands of man and of nature. For he, like Judas, is seeing only the three hundred shillings. One can become so "dead to rapture and despair" that for thirty pieces of silver he can betray the highest and best he has ever met.

In addition to his narrowness of vision, we find that Judas is dishonest. He kept the money bag and took from it; he was a thief. How hard it is for a man to erase the reputation he once establishes for himself! "For he was a thief," says John. Judas was in a predicament. He was moving in an environment of high ideals, of pure religion. How out-of-place were his thoughts and secret desires. He must conceal them, so he fits over his head the halo of charity. "This could have been sold and given to the poor." On another person this halo might have fitted well, but not on Judas. He perhaps thought by appearing concerned over the welfare of the poor, he was making an impression on Jesus and others. But hypocrisy fools no one but ourselves.

Now Judas is not an isolated person among all of human kind. Though we may not travel the full length of the road he selected, yet often we find ourselves on it.

Look at these similar instances. When Napoleon was busy rearranging the map of Europe to suit his fancy, leaving thousands of dead bodies wherever his ambition traveled, did he speak of it as greed or love of power? He said he was bringing French liberty to the world. When Mussolini bludgeoned the terror-stricken natives of Ethiopia into a helpless, submissive pulp, what did he say was his purpose? It was to civilize the Ethiopians!

As we pursue the thought which this text suggests, we find that it comes uncomfortably close to ourselves. Sometimes we, too, try to put a halo over us that fits rather awkwardly. Now and then we sit about in circles and dissect another's reputation and pass to others stray bits of gossip and piously indulge in this character-destroying process, while we wrap our remarks in unctuous phrases such as: "Isn't it terrible?" and "Isn't it too bad?"—implying that we are without flaw.

We now and then give to our acts a halo of righteousness. We drive a hard bargain and call it good business. We selfishly hold to our earthly goods and begrudgingly share with others, and call it being economical. We sometimes assume a lone-wolf attitude toward the human pack. But do we speak of our non-co-operative attitude as stubbornness? No, it has the lofty title of conviction!

When we neglect obvious duties at home or elsewhere, do we call it indifference? Rather, we lend to ourselves an air of importance: we carry the world upon our shoulders, we are too busy, we are occupied with other weightier matters and can not be disturbed by little things.

The man who squanders his money loves to think of himself as popular and a good fellow.

Our ego is ever on the defensive, and as soon as we appear vulnerable at one point, the mind thrusts forth a defense in the form of a sword shaped like a virtue, but it is a sword that is made of paper. Every shade of evil, every evil plan carries with it a halo to conceal its true nature. Many a gesture of courtesy, many an expression of devotion, of sympathy, conceals behind it an evil purpose. How often the shadow of Judas falls across our words and actions!

Of this black side of human nature Jesus was fully aware. No one knew the deceitful motives and the treacherous thoughts of human beings as well as Jesus, and yet he had faith in their redemption. He believed that however low a man may sink in hypocrisy, he can come out of it. No matter how entangled a man is in graft, and troubles, and fears, he can work his way out.

The first sign that God is working on you in seeking to rid you of that sin is your becoming aware of its existence. Half the battle is won when you see it, when you admit its presence.

Here are a few suggestions. Associate with Christian people. They may not be as flashy as some friends you have, but their moral integrity will make hypocrisy difficult. Choose the right. Judas moved in the best environment possible, yet he did not choose the right. You must with determination follow the guidance of God.

Cultivate the Christian habit of being honest with yourself, of going directly at any irritating problem, and first at the personal part of the equation.

Content yourself with minor rôles in the drama of life. Perhaps you seek always to hold the center of the stage, and by a pretense of knowledge and skill you seek to maintain that place.

Above all, see if your aims in life, both great and small, are Christian. If they are, if they are acceptable to God in the light of the Bible and the example of Jesus, you may be sure your transparent goodness and sincerity will bring upon you the respect and love of your fellow men and the blessing of God.

Do as Sir William Osler, who said: "Each night I not only unclothe myself, but undress my soul in the presence of God and bring my thinking in tune with the mind of Christ!"

V. THE GREATEST NEED TODAY

. . . and the forest devoured more people that day than the sword devoured. 2 Samuel 18. 8.

THIS passage from the Old Testament is a strange description of a battle which took place in the forest of Ephraim. Absalom had revolted against his father David. The forces of father and son met in a fierce battle, and at the close of the day, when they began to count their losses, they found that thousands had been slain, but to their amazement they learned that more had been devoured by the forest than had been slain by the sword. Their greatest loss had not been actual combat with spear and sword, but from those who had become lost in the forest. It may be that many of them sought the jungle as a way of escape, others were probably devoured by the animals, some wandered aimlessly about trying to find their way out to the open fields, but whatever the cause, more were devoured by the forest than were slain by the sword.

In this discovery of the cause of most of their losses is a symbolic truth, a truth that is as valid today as it was then. The forest still devours more than are slain by the sword. In the battle of life more people are brought low by indecision, lack of direction, aimless wandering about and never following a clearly outlined road, than by actual combat with life. If we were to check the lives of a hundred men whose days came to a close without any worthy contribution to this world, I think we would find that the majority of them just wandered from path to path, from job to job, from place to place, and all the while the clock was ticking off their years, and before they realizde it, their time was up. They were not slain by actual combat with life, with temptations and burdens, but they drifted on and off the scene.

The battle scene referred to was part of the bloody revolution led by Absalon. Our age, too, is one of revolution; perhaps bloodless revolution as far as we are concerned, but we live in an age of revolution, nevertheless. Other parts of the world are finding their changes coming by the shedding of blood (Russia, Germany, Italy, Japan, Spain), but so far, whatever changes have taken place in this country in recent years have been peaceful, although not without suffering.

Before 1914, and one might move the date up to 1920, people moved along set and rigid lines.

They were knit together in small units, bound in one group geographically or nationally. As a result, customs, habits, ideals, religions were frequently determined by the caste or group into which one was born. You heard about other communities, other places, ideas, but they were far distant and had nothing to do with your own conduct.

Then came mass production, the spread of good roads; the automobile put the nation on wheels, and soon we were intermingling with others and exchanging our separate heritages. Words and pictures sent as if by magic from one end of the globe to the other broke down the boundary lines that held us rigidly in our groove. Instead of following the beaten tracks morally, spiritually, and socially, we found ourselves in a maze of new and untried roads. We found ourselves in a forest with no marked highways, in a situation with no clear-cut answer as to what is right and what is wrong. Today respectable and learned people defend or oppose that which but a few years ago was reversely denounced or upheld. Which path is the one to take?

Twenty years ago when a young man of fifteen came to manhood, he arrived with a definite set of rules of conduct, a clear idea as to what road he should travel. He may not have gone that road, but he had no doubt in his mind that it was the road he should go. The young man coming up to life today has no such fixed path before him. Employment is uncertain, pleasures and entertainment are highly commercialized and therefore fraught with much danger, and ideals, morals, and religion are not very deeply set into his nature. He comes to a forest of uncertainty, and when the losses are counted, we find that more of our younger generation are devoured by the forest than are slain by the sword.

What is needed in this age, and in any age that has these characteristics of confusion, erased lines, and no marked roads to the open plains?

To get out of the forest we need Christian leaders, men who not only know what they are talking about, but who are actuated by the highest motives. We need saintly old people.

But as soon as I use the word old, you think of someone who is seventy or over. You picture a man bent with age and giving advice about the way he used to live with an I-told-you-so comment. I mean, however, a person who has kept learning, growing, observing and adding to his knowledge of God and man. Age enters in. Very few young men can qualify. It takes time and thought. I am thinking especially of the people from forty-five and up. It is from this group that we must get our leaders.

You have heard it said that this is an age of youth. It ought not to be. For it is but common sense to know that if a man has been growing mentally and spiritually, he is of much more value at the age of forty-five and fifty-five and over than at twenty-five and thirty-five.

But it is not enough to be old in experience.

Age is not sufficient. In the Old Testament we are told that Methuselah lived so many years, and then died. He was just old. Life requires more than age and experience. It is a matter of attitude toward life. The degrees that a man may have after his name, the books he may have written, do not determine whether or not he is to be trusted. That is determined by the direction he wants to go, and he himself is going. What is the right attitude toward life? I call it the saintly attitude.

Immediately when we use the word saintly, we think of a person who is almost flawless in conduct, free from outward vice, who has a piety that is unattractive and unapproachable. There has come down through the ages a false idea of what a saint really is. If a man moved with a ponderous step and held away from his fellow men and spoke in heavy tones and avoided smiling, such a man was often spoken of as "saintly." I believe, however, that saintly people are those persons who have passed through the many woods of life and have not been lost in any one of them, who have endured sorrow and not become melancholy, who have laughed and not given way to frivolity, who have met ruthless treatment by supposed friends and not given way to bitterness. Those are the people we need today, and no doubt that is the great need in every generation. There are plenty of elderly people ready to give advice with papal finality, but too few saintly old people who are tolerant, strong, patient, and helpful.

Fortunate is the young man who numbers among his friends a saintly old person. Such a friendship existed between Paul and Timothy— Paul, the intrepid, weather-beaten missionary, and Timothy, the young and uncertain Christian. Can you not hear the two in a conversation, Timothy saying, "Paul, I can't seem to make any headway; the problems are too great for me; if I had your ability and experience, or a better education, I might accomplish something for the Kingdom." Then I see the saintly old Paul put his hand on the shoulder of Timothy and firmly and kindly say: "Timothy, Timothy, stir up the gift of God that is in you, for God gave us not a spirit of fear, but of power and love and discipline."

When young we seldom watch where the arrows will fall. We say and do things never bothering as to consequences. Injuries to others, hurt feelings do not disturb us much. In our ignorance of values, we push and shove at the counters of life, greedily reaching for what we want, careless as to how we handle articles which do not belong to us. Experience and intelligence should make us more considerate. Not only more considerate, but also more patient with others.

There is a certain harshness and ruthlessness about us when we are young. Age should mellow a person. A greedy old man is always repulsive. When we see an old person measuring this life in terms of dollars and cents, by how much he can get out of it, we know that that person has nothing to teach us. For if any one should know the limits of money, it should be an aged person.

I think a saint should be slow to condemn. It is, of course, easy to forgive someone who has not offended you. It requires no great amount of Christian grace to excuse the sins of another if those sins have not hurt you. But I am speaking of sins that cause *you* to suffer, due to the carelessness, selfishness, and ignorance of others. Some in this world must be the shock absorbers. Blows are going to be struck, and our first inclination is to pass them on to others, but we should bear the blows silently. In this world mean things are going to be said; old people should be above passing them on. Saintly old people should love their fellow men in spite of their shortcomings. Bad temper, revengeful spirits, and meannesses do not become a saintly old person.

But every virtue has its vice running parallel to it, and the ripeness of age always carries with it the possibility of decay. The virtue of mellowness often moves into the vice of spinelessness. Saintly old people must not only be forgiving, but that forgiving, patient attitude is not to rise from feebleness. You must stand for something. We may smile at the rigid rules that our forefathers abided by, but they did stand for certain principles, and they were willing to risk their lives in their defense. We may disagree with them as to their principles, but we can not disagree with them as to the rightness of standing for some standard.

At a national convention of a certain insurance company, a doctor told this to the group: One day he had been taken before the court for speeding. The judge asked him if he had been hurrying to a case. Here was his chance; he could easily have said yes. A host of friends would have patted him on the back for being clever, but something prompted him to tell the truth, and he paid the fine. When he came home, he thought he had been something of a fool, until his boy said to him: "Daddy, I was proud of you today!" "Why?" asked the father. "Because you did not tell a lie to save twenty-five dollars," the boy answered. That father received many times over the value of the money, because he was honest. How many men are there like that today? An insurance agent said to me that of all the tires stolen from automobiles, he did not know of a single case where it was not a *new* (?) tire. I have known people to push an insurance claim to the last ounce of silver in it. Such men can not qualify as saintly old people; they will be of no help to us in finding our way through the forest of uncertainty.

There is another quality that saintly people should have—they should retain the freshness and vigor of youth. How quickly our alertness is dulled by time. How easily we substitute platitudes and the free giving of advice for thinking! Plenty of old people stop their influence by losing the listening ear.

Some old people think they are not wanted in this world merely because they are old. No, the reason that many persons are shelved is that they have fallen back on the attitude expressed by the phrase: "I ought to know; I have had that experience!" I think of a mother who asked me to mention in a funeral sermon that children should be obedient to parents and listen to them. A good thought, but her children would hardly obey her because I said so in a sermon. She must stand on her own feet and by her own character win their respect and obedience.

How delightful old people can be when they have kept a fresh, eager interest in life. When a person comes up to old age with not just years behind him, when he still has the attitude of searching and learning and listening, it is a joy to come in contact with him. I met such a man a few summers ago. It was a delight to visit with him. Edwin Markham was then over eighty, but his mind was alert, his laugh was as contagious as that of a youngster, his ideals were polished, and not broken by trial. When he learned that I was a minister, he said: "If you were to cut my heart open, in the center you would find Jesus Christ!"

That is the need of our generation, and of any generation: saintly old people. Whatever forest we run into in society or religion, we must depend on the leadership in high and low places of those who are older and wiser and who possess Christlike ideals. It is this age that has collapsed. Two things have robbed us of that leadership. The war killed off ten million men, and no doubt among them were many possible leaders. But much more by far than the war, the cushioned years from 1920 to 1930 weakened the spine, the morals, the character of men who were thirty-five years and over. Vanity, easy money, soft living broke them, and now they have not the leadership qualities necessary.

Upon you men and women who are forty-five years and over rests the burden of leadership. You ar ethe leaders; you are the men and women to lead the way out of the forest. I am not speaking now about geniuses. I refer to ordinary people who in the circle in which they live must cast a light that is steady and clear.

When Gideon rose to the leadership of Israel, he looked about him and the weakness of the nation made him ask: "Where are the mighty men who lived in the days of our fathers?" What I have been saying is that the leadership of this world must be in the hands of Christian men and women who move in the light, for as Jesus said: "He that followeth me shall not walk in darkness." Our leaders must be in that light!

BE MERCIFUL unto me, O God—forgive my failure to reveal in my daily conduct the mind and compassion of Jesus. Jealousy, bad temper, smug complacency, indifference, shallow thinking, greed—for these sins I seek Thy pardoning grace. Cleanse me from hidden weaknesses, give me courage to face the truth as Thou dost see the truth. Be merciful O God, unto me, a sinner.

Give to me an awareness of Thy presence.

When temptations crowd about me, when sorrow envelops me in darkness and loneliness, when doubt chills my faith, help me to keep my mind stayed on Thee that I might be kept in perfect peace—though the outward world be in turmoil, within shall be the calm which the Master revealed and promised to His followers, "My peace I give unto you."

Create within me a grateful heart, rejoicing always in Thy unfailing goodness. I thank Thee for daily bread, for food and shelter, for home and friends and above all for the revelation of Thyself in Jesus Christ. Whatever my experiences—joy or anguish, triumph or adversity, though my body be broken on the anvil of life, yet may I with my whole heart say, "All things work together for good to them that love the Lord."

Keep my Christian faith from becoming just lip service. Open mine eyes to the needs of my fellow men. Make me to have a sensitive ear to the cry of those who grope in darkness, who are in the bondage of fear, sin, and ignorance.

In my relationship with others through the church, the home, and the community, I pray for a spirit of ready helpfulness, for honesty and a forgiving heart.

Deepen my spiritual habits and broaden my Christian sympathies, so that when the rains descend and the floods gather, and the winds beat upon my soul, it shall stand firm on the eternal Rock, Jesus Christ.

It is in His name and spirit that I offer this prayer.   Amen.

The Grace of Our Lord Jesus Christ

CONRAD BERGENDOFF

THE GRACE OF OUR LORD JESUS CHRIST

I. THE KNOWLEDGE OF SIN

For I had not known. Romans 7. 7.

ALL mankind stands under the judgment of the cross. Its shadow lies over every human heart, for it is a judgment upon the sin of the world. If there were no sin, there would be no cross of Christ. All our Lenten observance is meaningless and hollow unless we take seriously the fact of sin. As men stumbling in dark places come unexpectedly up against a barrier which strikes them with its very suddenness and strangeness, so that they involuntarily exclaim, "What's this?", so to the average man and woman plodding on in the murky light of daily routine, the cross unexpectedly towers before them, and the half-startled, half-irritated response is "What's this?" What is this frequently heard talk in Lent about a cross? Who is this Crucified One? What does it concern me?

As silently and as stubbornly as a shadow, the message of the cross stabs through our human life. It proclaims that all is not well with us. Like a two-edged sword, it pierces our complacency, our smug satisfaction, our clever self-deceit, and says to the inmost heart, "You are unhappy. Your life is miserable. You are trying to make your-

self believe that you are your own master." And
when we turn away from this voice, and comfort
ourselves by the thought, "I am as good as any
one else. I do the best I can. I have my own life
to live," the Crucified One persists, "If we say
we have no sin, we deceive ourselves, and the
truth is not in us."

Again I say if we mean to take Lent seriously,
it will not all be a pleasant business. It will be
something else than beautiful music, hushed sanc-
tuaries, the comfortable feeling of being one of
the multitudes that throng holy places to keep
holy festivities. The cross will have to come down
from steeple or altar and come very near to our
own thoughts and feelings. Nor will carrying it
around our necks be the same as carrying it in
our hearts. There is something very personal
about Lent. "My body," said Christ, was "broken
for you," "My blood was shed *for you*." The
message goes straight home, if it goes at all. It is
not to the crowds, not to your neighbor, but to *you*
that He who was on the cross, wishes to speak.
There is no referring of the matter to a commit-
tee, or a secretary, or a friend. The cross stands
athwart my path—what am I to do about it?

My answer to that question is simply this: for
once, be silent and know that He who speaks
from the cross is God. For once stop your chatter whereby you try to cover up the awful void
of your soul. Be quiet and let Him speak. For
there is a word from the cross if only we had
ears to hear. The noise of the world is so much

stronger that you will have to come pretty close. On the first Good Friday the crowds flowed past Him. They cheered, and they jeered, they scoffed, they asked curious questions. Only a small, silent group at the cross heard what He said. The others either heard nothing or misunderstood what they did hear. If you would catch some meaning from the event, leave the crowd, and stand humbly with Mary, John, and the other disciples. Perchance some word from His lips may reach your heart.

Only that group, I believe, sense the significance of the cross. The world of the Greeks, the Romans, the Jews, did not understand it. "Foolishness," the Greeks described it. "A stumbling-block"—something hard to get over—the Jews said. "Superstition" the learned of all ages have deemed it. Do not believe that the band at the foot of the cross will ever be a popular one. If you are waiting for a majority vote to determine where you are to stand, you need not be in much doubt. Those who crucify Him can hardly be expected to do other than mock Him. The mockery may be brutal and gross. That is the modern Russian way. It may be insolent, as is the way with modern Teutonic pagans. Or it may be cynical, sophisticated, in the manner of the so-called modern intelligentsia. There are many means of torture, and Christ has suffered all man's inventions whereby they seek to get rid of Him. All the while they seek to silence Him, they publish

abroad their lack of faith in Him and of understanding the will of God.

For the shadow of the cross is the obverse side
of a light which comes from another source. The
Crucified One speaks of another kind of life, of
another kingdom, in another language. Here is
"revealed the power of God unto salvation," wrote
an apostle who had come to understand the meaning of the cross. The cross speaks of "God," "salvation," "revelation"—words which are not common currency in daily life. Therefore the multitudes will pass it by with a shrug of the shoulder,
a witty remark, or fatal indifference. But to those
who seek the meaning of life and are concerned
about a peace of heart as well as holiness of character, there is a magnetic appeal in Him who,
lifted up, draws unto Himself all who care for the
truth. "I had not known sin, but by the law," ex-
claimed Paul. The cross is the end of the law, and
in its light we see ourselves as He sees us. Then
indeed our only cry is, "Lord, have mercy upon
me, a sinner."

II. The Guilt of Sin

Himself took our infirmities, and bare our diseases.
Matthew 8. 17.

SOMETIMES people have been anxious about
the site of the cross. Considerable effort has
been expended in locating the exact place where
Christ was crucified. In a deeper sense, we need

not look very far. For we might say that the
cross is rooted in the guilt of man. Wherever
there is sin, the grace of God is seeking the sinner. And the foundation on which the cross rests
is as deep as the direct sin. The arms of the Crucified One embrace all the generations of mankind. The feet of Christ rest on an earth where
our human lives are touched by all the infirmities of sin.

But where is the source of sin? This question
is both an ancient and an ever modern one. In
all ages men have tried to place the responsibility
for their weaknesses in their bodily selves, seeking to excuse themselves because of their earthly
natures. They have wanted to say that our minds
are pure, only our bodies impure. Our intentions,
they have claimed, are good, only because of the
weakness of our bodies, we fail to realize them.
Sin, some would say, is in fact nothing but a
weakness for which we can not be blamed. Our
better selves are our minds, our souls. These are
in the image of God. These are free. We can forget our sordid, failing, bodily selves. We are the
captains of our souls. We are the master of our
destiny.

Now this is all very modern—and very, very
ancient. A European writer[1] has recently made
very clear that in the early Christian centuries
the church had to fight stoutly to defend itself
against a heresy which took three forms. The

---

[1] NYGREN, A. *Eros and Agape*, Vol. 2.

wise Greeks did not like to accept the Christian
teaching that God created the earth. They were
willing to admit that God was in the heavens, but
not that He had anything to do with physical,
material things. He could me concerned only with
spiritual forms and beings. That was one point.
A second was similar. These cultured pagans
could not understand how God could become man.
For God to be born of the Virgin Mary, to possess
a real, true human body, that was unthinkable
to their clever, educated, minds. And the third
point at which they rebelled was the teaching of
the resurrection of the body. That the souls of
the dead might live again they thought they could
understand. But to them it was rank superstition
to talk about the resurrection of the *body.* Yet
the church won out in the controversy. Today
each time you and I repeat the Creed we bear
witness to that victory of the gospel over the
learned unbelievers of the first few centuries, for
we still say, "I believe in God the Father Almighty, maker of heaven and *earth;* "I believe in Jesus
Christ, *born* of the Virgin Mary," and "I believe
in the resurrection of the dead," that is, body as
well as soul.

Why do I bring you back to those ancient days?
For this reason—to illustrate how hard it is for
us mortals to realize that we are both body and
spirit, so that we can not separate the two and
say that our sin is in our bodies but not in our
spirits. God has united mind and matter, and
what He has united, let no one seek to separate.

No, our guilt is not in one part, here or there, in our bodies, or in our thoughts, or in our intentions. Our guilt is in our very being, and to help us God Himself had to take on human, mortal frame, to bear our iniquities, and carry our infirmities. That makes Him one with us. He has entered our sinful existence, and planted His cross just where we are. Where our foulest deeds are, where man's deepest guilt lies, there you will find the foot of the cross.

You will find the cross arising, too, out of man's deepest need. And that need is where? Let us be perfectly frank, and not seek to dodge the issue. Man's most insistent need is an answer at the grave. Death is as real as anything in life. Sooner or later there must be an answer. I have read many fine words about a noble attitude toward death, but they have come from men and women who have taken many years to learn that attitude. Very baldly stated, we fear death. We resist death. We do not even want to talk about dying. And all the while it is a fact toward which each day brings us irresistibly. I am convinced that the dread with which men regard death is connected very closely with the consciousness of guilt which grows out of their life. They are afraid to face God. Like the first sin, all our sins drive us to seek to hide ourselves from the presence of God. Death brings us into His presence. Even the denial of God is largely an attempt on the part of those who make it to escape from Him. There is no "ending of it all," there is no "getting away from" either God or our guilty selves. Death is the great valley of shadow, whose shadow falls over all of life. Any religion which denies death, or has nothing to say in its presence, is a most inadequate, nay, a very false religion. But it is right here that the cross stands—outside the city gates, at the end of all the life which centers there. Here it stands in the Place of the Skull, the emblem of death to body and mind. Here in man's most darksome grief, here in the hour when all earthly clamor is hushed, stands the rod and staff which give comfort to those who pass through the valley of the shadow of death.

Where man's deepest distress, his most awful need, and his most ineradicable guilt meet, at those crossroads is a cross from which comes the promise of life and redemption.

III. THE FORGIVENESS OF SIN

God was in Christ reconciling the world unto himself.
2 Corinthians 5. 19.

IN the history of the Christian church we find that its teachers have been reluctant to speak of the suffering of God the Father. Something there is which causes us to draw back from ascribing our own most common experiences to the Almighty. Can God suffer pain? Can He know anguish of spirit? We have been unwilling to say yes to such questions. It has been easier for us to think of Christ experiencing the torture of the cross, for was not He true man? But in doing so, we have, probably unknowingly, separated the human from the divine in Christ and thought only of the human nature as suffering.

But the more one ponders the mystery of the cross, the more one feels that what the Scripture says is just this: God suffered. I know that it is much easier to understand the sufferings of man than the suffering of God. Jesus, however, has helped us by a parable which is one of the simplest yet one of the most profound of all the parables.

You remember the story of the prodigal son. Who, in fact, once he has heard it, can ever forget it? But perhaps your attention has been absorbed by the prodigal, out there among the swine, longing for some of their food to fill his own need. We grasp quite readily the sensations connected with hunger. Or we think of his loss of friends, his dirty garments, his homesickness even, which began to overpower him. I do not say that we have overemphasized that portion of the picture, for it is well that we paint in striking colors the wages of sin. But there is another figure which is in the deeper background, whose emotions are less often studied. It is the Father, who is waiting at home for the return of his boy. Parents will understand better than children what that means. Compare, if you can, the pain and suffering experienced by parents whose children have gone wrong with the anxiety and agony of that Father. It is my conviction that the

Father's grief is far more bitter than the sorrow which the physical misfortunes of the children cause earthly parents. There are scars in the souls of parents which never heal, and the sins of children are like thrusts of a sword into the hearts of a mother or father whose whole life has been one of love to an erring child. The sleepless nights, the days of mortification, the years which bring no hope or healing—ah, we know little of that type of suffering because in most cases it is silently borne, even carefully concealed, and sometimes brings closer the death of the parent in whose heart the burden is as a millstone.

If I were to put the mystery of the cross into the simplest terms I know how, I think it would be in this manner: The sins of His children broke the heart of God. For two reasons I would describe it thus. For one thing, we know something of the pain and unutterable grief which causes a heart to break. And for another, this simile points to the motive that brought God to the terrible ordeal of Calvary. It was not necessary for Him so to suffer, for the Creator of the ends of the earth could have hurled his perverted creatures to their doom. Or He could have forsaken them, and left them to the consequences of their arrogance. But no. Even as a father pities his children, so this Father through Christ sought to win His children back to the Father's house. Not with force—He compels none. But with the silent power of His love He draws them. On Himself He takes all their sins. He carries their burdens.

He suffers the consequences of their guilt. He dies for them whose sin had earned the wages of death. On the cross Christ died of a heart broken by the ingratitude, the selfishness, the pride, the hatred of those He would save even as a mother hen would gather her chicks underneath her wings. It was the supreme act of God's mercy. And those who are not won by it? Heaven and earth know no other way to win them—they are lost.

Out of the gloom of that day of crucifixion has come a ray of light which in all succeeding centuries has gladdened the hearts of believers. It is the light of faith in a God who forgives the sins of men and women who would go even so for as to seek to get rid of their God. The worst that man can do can not quench the love of God. But it is a part of the revelation of the cross that this love of God costs dearly. Men sometimes speak of that love as if it were a very cheap thing —it cost God nothing. As if the nature of God's love were one that paid no attention to the sins of men, but overlooked everything. Not so does God love. That kind of sentiment may be in our hearts as we close our eyes to the errors of our fellow men, and say, it does not matter. It does matter. Nothing in all the world is more terribly real than the consequences and the guilt of sin. These can not be gotten rid of by easy attitudes or empty words. The love of God is a love which suffers deeply and bitterly. It rejoiceth not, as Paul says, in iniquity. It is a holy love, and no man teaches truly the Word of God who emphasizes the love of God at the expense of his holiness and righteousness.

We are bought with a price. In anguish of spirit which man never can understand, God paid the price of our iniquity. The grace of our Lord Jesus Christ is a forgiving grace, but won only by the sacrifice of Himself. The world will not understand, but pass unheeding by. Only the grateful, penitent sinner will realize that because He died we may live. Never will we get very far from the cross. This is the source and fountain of all our righteousness. The cross of Christ is the meeting place where God meets man.

IV. THE GRACE-FILLED LIFE

It is no longer I that live, but Christ liveth in me. Galatians 2. 20.

IF we would know the true meaning and power of the Crucified Christ, we will find part of the answer in the life of the individual Christian. There is a pathetic note in the search of some people for God. They seek Him in history, or archaeology, in science, or even in theology, but never find Him. Sometimes one wonders if they are really in earnest, or if they are not more interested in the search than in God. For sometimes they pass Him by, and do not recognize Him when they see Him. In their search they go right on past the place where He has said He is to be found. Are they really seeking God or seeking the kind of god they want? It is an ancient practice, for long ago the prophet complained, "They have forsaken me and sought for other gods."

When one seeks in order to find, one follows the guidance of those who have found, not of those who do not know. We do well to turn a deaf ear to all the dubious and doubting teachers of our generation who can ask thousands of questions but give no answer to the cry of the soul. Recall often those stanzas from one of the oldest of Christian hymns:

> If I ask Him to receive me,
>   Will He say me nay?
> "Not till earth and not till heaven
>   Pass away."
>
> Finding, following, keeping, struggling,
>   Is He sure to bless?
> "Saints, apostles, prophets, martyrs,
>   Answer, 'Yes.'"

Not in daily newspapers, or modern periodicals, very often not in current books, or over the radio, will you find the Christ of the cross. Be not discouraged if these know nothing about Him. Go rather to those who do know Him. Seek Him in His Word, where He may be found. There you will learn to know what is the nature of life at the cross.

Christians in all ages have testified to the peculiar place the cross has in their experience of

Him. You might compare it to the compass of the mariner. Wherever he sails, far or near, his needle points always to the north. In all the vicissitudes of Christian experience, be they events of joy or grief, success or failure, somehow all point to Him who seems to have made the cross His throne and the center of His activity. Even in the Book of Revelation where Christ's heavenly position is described you recall that He is pictured as the Lamb that was slain.

What is this strange power of the Crucified One to transform human characters? Why is it that if a soul approaches Him, that soul is never again the same? These are questions that can not in this life ever be fully answered. But some parts of the answer have come to us from "saints, apostles, prophets, martyrs."

The most remarkable thing that happens at the cross, I believe, is the turning of a person from himself to the Christ who here speaks. That turning point men call conversation, and the word means just that—a turning. Before that experience, oneself has been the supreme ruler, and one's own interests have ruled all thoughts and actions. After that experience, the words of Paul become real, "It is no longer I that live, but Christ liveth in me." Christ has come to be the Master of the heart. Henceforth all of life turns toward Him.

Words to tell why this happens are difficult to find. But two words I have found helpful. The power of Christ which He exercises from the cross the church has agreed to call grace. And grace, Luther clearly taught us, is the same as the forgiveness of sins. The grace of our Lord Jesus Christ is His forgiving of our sins. To live in grace is to be in that relationship which we call faith, and to have continuously the experience that in Him we have the forgiveness of sin. Somehow grace and the cross are inseparable. At the cross we find grace, and since in this life we ever need forgiveness, the cross becomes the center of our spiritual life, from which we never get very far. There we have found Him who does for us what no one else can do.

One of the words is *grace*. The other is *gratitude*. And gratitude is the soul's response to the miracle of the Crucified One. You might call it faith. That is the classic word. I would add this word only because we seem to have forgotten that faith includes joy and thanksgiving. It is out of gratitude to Christ that we do His will, and the attitude of our minds and hearts is this thankfulness. The grace-filled life is the grateful life.

The celebration of the Lord's Supper is a high point in the observance of Holy Week. There we enter into His fellowship and into the events of the night in which He was betrayed. To receive the gifts of the Lord's Supper we need faith. But let us not forget that an early Christian name for this feast was Eucharist, which means thanksgiving. Maundy Thursday is a spiritual Thanksgiving Day. Its significance includes this, that in the Christian who meets the present Christ there is created by the Spirit a new heart, where thankfulness to Him takes the place of service to self. From the cross goes a new creature whose desires, ambitions, love have all been transformed. Life from that point is lived in the presence of the crucified Christ. "I am crucified with Christ: nevertheless I live—and the life which I now live in the flesh I live by the faith of the Son of God, who loved me, and gave himself for me."

V. The Fellowship of Grace

That ye may be able to comprehend with all saints.
Ephesians 3. 18.

THE Lord's Prayer nowhere uses the singular person in its references to those who thus pray. The very first word is "Our"—"*Our* Father." In its petitions it is "us" and "ours"—"Give *us our* daily bread," "Forgive *us, as we* forgive," "Lead *us,*" "Deliver *us.*" How different that prayer would be if you or I prayed, "My Father," "Give me," "Lead" and "Deliver me"! The most universally used prayer of Christianity in this very use of its pronouns tells us what so much else in Scripture tells us, that the Christian faith is a social faith, that Christianity is a fellowship or community, and not a solitary, private matter. If our religion be a thing all by itself it is not Christianity. He who only uses the first-person pronoun in his prayers has not learned the Lord's Prayer.

It is not out of place to emphasize this fact as we stand at the foot of the cross. Long ago a young man saw himself standing before the throne of God. As the vision of God's holiness opened up before him, he gave expression to the feeling which stirred the depths of his being. "Woe is me!" he cried. "I am a man of unclean lips, and I dwell in the midst of a people of unclean lips." And in the dawn of the New Testament day, the ancient Simeon cried out, as he beheld the Promised One, "Mine eyes have seen thy salvation, which thou hast prepared before the face of all people." It is a part of the miracle of the cross that those who find there a new relationship to God find at the same time a new attitude toward their fellow men. Out of the cross of Christ grows the Church of Christ, the communion or fellowship of the saints.

The redemption of Christ is the redemption of a people. Of course He brings His message directly to the heart of the individual, and the entrance to His kingdom is so narrow that we may enter only singly, one by one. But entering into the kingdom is the beginning of a life which expresses itself in social relationships. The love of God which is shed abroad in our hearts by Christ Jesus is a love which goes out to our fellow men. The grace which we have spoken of as calling forth the gratitude of the believers is the love of God dwelling in the hearts of the Christians and creating a whole new world of human relationships. This community of Christians with

Christ and with one another is the church which the New Testament does not hesitate to call the body of Christ.

There is a sense in which this body of Christ is still being mocked, despised, crucified in the world of today. Possibly such an example as the attempt of Russia to annihilate the church comes most readily to mind. But we need not go outside our own nation, or community, or even our own circle of associations, to find many an attempt to rid the world of the body of Christ and His Spirit. Any man or woman, young or old, who as a part of the church seeks to witness to the life that is in Christ, will experience that the process of the crucifixion still goes on. Christ bore the sins of the world. They who follow in His footsteps must bear the burden each generation places on the company of the Saviour. Anyone who succeeds in escaping this burden has deceived himself. Safe in his own secret or solitary Christianity, he has, ere he knew it, separated himself from the body of Christ.

Hypocrites there may be in the church. But whoever holds himself aloof from the church for that reason gives the world one more hypocrite. For one does not seek the church for its social advantages, but for what the church offers in spiritual treasures. These treasures are the light of the Word, the power of the sacraments, the strengthening of faith. For all of its brokenness, its weakness, its divisions, the church still is the bearer of the Spirit of God to mankind. I speak of no one denomination or group. I refer to the church as the teacher of God's Word, and the communion of those who have experienced the redemption of Christ. If in this church you do not find God, you will not find Him anywhere else in all the wide world.

Through a people, the fellowship of the church, faith in the Christ as the King of our lives is born. Through the church He would work His will in all the social relationships wherein we have a part. After Good Friday comes Easter, and the Ascension, and Pentecost. At the cross is born the community which after the gift of His Spirit has come goes out to evangelize all nations, revolutionizing man's dealings with fellow men, setting up a new hope for society in time and eternity.

It would be a tragedy if out of our observance of Holy Week we went again to our daily tasks with only memories. The recurring celebration of Lent is significant only if each time it strengthens us in our devotion to the Body wherein we have found our life and faith. We have but glimpsed anew some of the fragments of the truth which is in Christ. If ever we shall come to learn the length and the breadth, the height and the depth of the knowledge of God it will, as Paul tells us, be necessary that we "comprehend with all the saints." Out of a lifelong fellowship with Christians in the body of Christ we may see how far away are the horizons of His kingdom, horizons which extend far beyond the grave and this present order of things. The cross of Christ stands on vantage ground from which His people view the Promised Land to which their King does lead them.

Christ's Seven Words from the Cross

CHRIST'S SEVEN WORDS FROM THE CROSS

THE FIRST WORD

Father, forgive them; for they know not what they do.
Luke 23. 34.

"Beneath the cross of Jesus
I fain would take my stand,
The shadow of the mighty rock
Within a weary land;
A home within the wilderness,
A rest upon the way,
From burning of the noontide heat,
And burden of the day."

"HE was wounded for our transgressions, he was bruised for our iniquities." Thus spoke Isaiah the prophet seven hundred years before Christ and thirty-three years after Christ was born the prophecy was fulfilled. On a little hill called Golgotha, outside the wall of Jerusalem, Jesus the Son of Man who was called Christ the Son of God, the Messiah promised by God when man fell in sin, was nailed to a cross between two malefactors. The greatest crime committed in history. Thus did Christ the Son of God suffer the punishment for our sins, thus did He bear the sins of the world in His body on the cross. The cross was a tree of cursing and shame. Now to us Christians it is the sweetest word of all. We place the cross upon our altars and on the steeple

of our churches. It is a sign of great honor. In
holy baptism we received the sign of the cross
upon our brow and upon our breast as a token
that we should believe in the crucified Lord Jesus
Christ. With the sign of the cross we consecrate
the bread and wine in holy communion and with
it we finish the benediction. They pierced His
hands and feet with nails, but there was no bitterness, no resentment in His heart. He did not
curse those who cursed Him, He did not condemn
His tormentors. He had compassion on them, as
the Father had compassion on a fallen mankind,
"for God so loved the world, that he *gave* his only
begotten Son."

In the hour when He was rejected and despised
by His own people, betrayed, denied and forsaken
by His disciples, and tormented and executed by
cruel pagan soldiers, He prayed: "Father, forgive
them; for they know not what they do." In this
prayer we have the highest and most beautiful
expression of the Saviour's love. In 1 Cor. 13
Paul has given a most beautiful description of
the love that was crucified on Calvary, the love
that prayed: "Father, *forgive* them; for they
know not what they do." "Love divine, all love
excelling!" Only beneath the cross of Jesus can
man begin to comprehend this holy and divine
love. "O sacred head, now wounded, with grief
and shame weighed down, now scornfully surrounded with thorns, Thine only crown." And
still He prayed: "Father, forgive them!" All sin
must be forgiven before man can find salvation.

Even these perpetrators, these hypocrites, priests, and Pharisees, the rebel that cried: "Crucify, crucify!" they should be given an opportunity to repent, they did not know what they were doing. To the reason of the common man it seems unreasonable to excuse such injustice, such cruelty as was committed against the Son of God, but such was the love of Christ that He could overlook the ingratitude of His people, the fanaticism of the priests and scribes, the weakness of an unscrupulous judge and the barbarism of the Roman soldiers and pray: "Father, they know not what they are doing." The glory of Christ had been veiled, only occasionally His divinity appeared, when He healed the sick, stilled the storm, and fed the multitude, but otherwise in all appearance He was just a human being, a poor and humble teacher traveling through the country teaching and preaching, still they should have known—"he spoke as one who had authority and not as their scribes," He proclaimed the kingdom of God, He did His Father's works and fulfilled the prophecies. But they did not know, and He excused them because He loved them so. He still wanted to extend the time of grace. "Father, forgive them; for they know what they do." So great was God's love, "that he gave his Son," so great was the love of the Son, that He prayed even for those who nailed His love to the cross. And from that cross the loving forgiveness of God goes out to all.

Without forgiveness there is no salvation

neither for the hypocrite of a high priest, nor for the worldling of a Pontius Pilate, neither for Peter or any of His disciples, nor for you or me. That is why Christ our Highpriest interceded for us on the cross, for those who crucified Him and for all sinners who do not know what they do, even though they ought to know—and thus He still intercedes for all who have not yet repented their sins. What a wonderful message to a world in sin and steeped in crime, a world at war, a world in strife! Oh, that it may be written with flaming letters in the sky and in the heart of every sinner: Christ the Son of God and Saviour of man prays: "Father, forgive them; for they know not what they do!"

You can not convert the world by laws but only by love. The love of God cries out to the world lost in sin, in Christ's prayer: "Father, forgive!" In the Lord's Prayer we pray: "Father, forgive us!" That is the first stepping-stone to God's throne and to eternal life. It requires a humble and penitent heart to pray this little prayer right. If prayed with a contrite heart, it shall open unto us an eternity of peace and everlasting blessing, salvation for a soul that was steeped in sin but washed in the blood of Christ poured out on the cross of Calvary, "given and shed for the forgiveness of our sins." At every communion we remember His sacrifice and are assured of the forgiveness of all our sins. And whenever we pray: "Lord, have mercy upon me a sinner," His prayer is answered, His wish fulfilled.

But if we are true followers of Christ, if we truly have accepted and believe in the forgiveness of our sins as promised us in Holy Baptism, then God expects of us the loving, kind, and forgiving mind that was in Jesus Christ. It is easy to pray for ourselves, most every man does that, but to pray for our enemies, for those who harm us and persecute us, requires a love of the highest standard, a godly love that few have attained—most of us are still in the lower grades. You will never be at peace with God before you have made peace with man, with those who antagonize you and possibly hate you. Make peace with them, pray for them, forgive them, ask God's blessing upon them. Make the dying Saviour's prayer your prayer:

"Father, forgive them; for they know not what they do."

> With broken heart and contrite sigh,
> A trembling sinner, Lord, I cry:
> Thy pardoning grace is rich and free,
> O God, be merciful to me.
>
> I smite upon my troubled breast,
> With deep and conscious guilt oppressed,
> Christ and His cross my only plea:
> O God, be merciful to me.
>
> Far off I stand with tearful eyes,
> Nor dare uplift them to the skies,
> But Thou dost all my anguish see,
> O God, be merciful to me.

Nor alms, nor deeds that I have done,
Can for a single sin atone,
To Calvary alone I flee:
O God, be merciful to me.

And when redeemed from sin and hell,
With all the ransomed throng I dwell,
My raptured song shall ever be:
God has been merciful to me.

CORNELIUS ELVEN.

THE SECOND WORD

Today shalt thou be with me in Paradise. Luke 23. 43.

THESE words were not spoken to a mighty king, a noted scientist, or a great philanthropist, but to a dying thief. Had the standard been lowered, since such words were uttered to one who was paying for his errors with his life? It might be reasonable to draw such a conclusion. But remember, the Master who ate with sinners and publicans, who loved all mankind, but hated sin, did not change His attitude even in the moment of death. God uses His own standard by which He reaches His decisions. We are so apt to weigh the things that can be seen only, the large gift, the beautiful donated cathedral, the great edifices erected to alleviate human suffering or for educational purposes. These are great gifts for which we as a people should be very grateful. But even the motive which prompts such gifts may not be sufficient to bring forth from the Master's lips, words of eternal life which were imparted to the suffering, dying sinner hanging on a cross at the side of Jesus.

A penitent heart always touches the heart of God. The cry of being remembered coming from one who had lived in dishonesty and shame, who had, as Matthew and Mark relate, joined in reproaching Him, touched the loving heart of the Saviour. This thief was not worthy to be remembered. The promise received was totally undeserved. But Christ, who is always ready to forgive when penitent hearts cry for mercy, speaks the words of hope to the soul in anguish. Man may reshape and change what God has made, but only God can create. Man may have his own idea concerning eternity, but only Christ can open the door of Paradise.

What good had this robber done? Nothing, as far as we know. In his dying hour he was saved as a brand out of the burning, saved by grace. Here we truly evidence the truth of the words: "By grace are ye saved, through faith, and that not of yourselves; it is the gift of God." He casts no one away who comes to Him. Never has He turned His face from a single weary and sin-laden soul. No sin is so abominable that He can and will not gladly forgive it. The robber who asks for mercy brings this truth vividly to us. How gladly Christ would have turned to the other robber and extended the same promise to him, if he had desired it. How willingly He would have given the same words of hope to those who reviled Him. What good have we done? Why should we be remembered? Only because of the mercy and grace of our Lord and Master. On you and me, He will gladly pronounce absolution if we desire it.

What caused the robber to pray? Could Jesus truly be a king, He who was nailed to a cross? Was there any royal evidence? "If thou art the king of the Jews, save thyself," cried the soldiers. "He saved others—himself he can not save. He is the king of Israel! Let him now come down from the cross and we will believe on him," cried the Sanhedrists. "If thou art the king of the Jews," now became a direct blasphemous challenge. The impenitent thief takes up the jeer and says, "Art thou not the Christ? Save thyself and us." But in spite of all the jeers, we note the majestic calm in the attitude of the Saviour. Strange as it may be, it is said that generally those crucified would, as a rule, utter insults in return to those gathered to witness their suffering and death, as if thereby to seek revenge and relief in such outbursts. Jesus did not seek revenge. He sought their salvation.

The desire to insult the crowd was not now found in the penitent thief, as evidenced by his request to the Lord. The fear of God has taken possession of his heart, and realizing that Jesus was suffering for no guilt of His own, we find him rising to the height of faith, saying: "For we receive the due reward of our deeds; but this man hath done nothing amiss."

As he heard the hammer strokes driving the

nails through the quivering flesh, and witnessed
the agony which followed, yet seeing One who
prayed for His enemies and realizing that this
Man was innocent, all must have deepened his im-
pressions of the One to whom he turned his dying
head in prayer to be remembered. Perhaps in
his youth he had heard Isaiah 53 read in the synagogues, and now it could be possible that the
memory of the words, "He was wounded for our
transgressions, he was bruised for our iniquities;
the chastisement of our peace was upon him; and
with his stripes we are healed," painted the picture of the One who was crucified by his side. It
is He who was wounded for my transgressions.
It is He who was bruised for my iniquities. The
dark hour of Christ's humiliation seems to break
and emit a ray of divine light and glory. Jesus
had done nothing wrong. The Sanhedrin had
condemned Him to death. People stood around
the cross and reviled Him—yet in spite of all this,
the thief cries out, "Lord, remember me." Crucified, yet he calls Him Lord. Stripped of His
attire, he hails Him as a King, and a true King
He was.

As we contemplate Christ's suffering and death,
we often are filled with pity and only that. Truly
Christ was humiliated, He suffered and He died,
but as we note the words that came from His lips
as He was nailed to the cross, the curtain seems
to be raised and we catch a glimpse of His kingly
power and authority. Is it not the same creative
voice which was heard before the world's first

morning? "He commanded and they were created." Ps. 148. 5. It was not merely an echo of
one who was, but the great I AM speaking, whose
words still had creative power. "Today shalt thou
be with me in Paradise." The penitent thief
spoke of the future. Christ spoke of today. The
dying thief believed that He possessed a kingdom
where he as a thief could not enter. Christ's
words opened the kingdom for him. His words
were life to a dying soul. Such words, such a
promise only Christ could utter. We may not
fully understand the meaning of Paradise, but
the promise of being with Jesus is sufficient. He
is Life. To be with Him is eternal life.

Far removed from Calvary's hill, what chance
have we? Often we wish that we could be as near
to Christ as the dying thief. So frequently Christianity with all its claims seems so vague and un-
real to us, only stories of a suffering and dying
Christ and nothing more. Thank God, Calvary
still tells its story to dying sinners. The words
spoken to the sinner on the cross have not lost
their power. God's words are still creative. When
we acknowledge our sins, and realize that any
punishment meted out to us is due reward for our
deeds, we may turn our heads to Christ and pray,
"Lord, remember me," as did the penitent thief.
The words of hope spoken to a dying sinner nearly two thousand years ago, are words of hope to
you and me today. Today He pleads for sinners
to come to Him. Today He still forgives all our

sins. He is the same yesterday, today, and forever.

Man may turn with his guilt and sin to sources which make him forget for a while, but forgetting is not forgiveness, forgetting is not removing our sins. But he who turns to Christ with his burden of sin will receive the same kind promise as did the robber on the cross. May His Holy Spirit work faith in our hearts to the end that we may receive from Christ forgiveness of sin, hope, peace, joy and life eternal. Today is your day and mine. Today is filled with God's grace and love. His outpoured spirit would lead us all to Calvary, where we, too, may hear the words of promise of being with Him today and forever—life eternal.

> Oh, come and stand beneath the cross
> And hear what Jesus speaks to us;
> The words that from His mouth proceed
> Will comfort us in times of need.
>
> O Jesus, pray Thou, too, for me
> That I increase my strength in Thee,
> My heart is weak, my eyes are blind,
> But grant that I Thy light may find.
>
> O Jesus, should I suffer loss
> And stand forsaken with my cross,
> Yea, even scorned by man I be,
> Send friends of Thine to comfort me.
>
> The robber who his sins confessed
> Found comfort in his Saviour blest,
> Who took the sting of death away
> And opened paradise for aye.

Oh, let me, too, when death is near,
From Thine own lips with gladness hear
The blessed words: "Come thou to be
Today in Paradise with me."

Almighty God, we thank Thee that Thou didst send Thine only begotten Son into this world in order that we, believing in Him, may have life eternal. Amen.

The Third Word

Woman, behold thy son! . . . Behold thy mother! John 19. 26–27.

MY friends, let us dedicate these few minutes to the Son of God, who was delivered for our offenses and raised again for our justification. To Him be glory and honor, now and forevermore. Our text is written in the 19th chapter of the Gospel according to John, verses 25 to 27: "Now there stood by the cross of Jesus his mother, and his mother's sister, Mary the wife of Cleophas, and Mary Magdalene. When Jesus therefore saw his mother, and the disciple standing by, whom he loved, he saith unto his mother, Woman, behold thy son! Then saith he to the disciple, Behold thy mother! And from that hour the disciple took her unto his own home."

Let us approach the scene of the crucifixion and join the first church of Christ to meet beneath the cross. Upon it hangs the church's Lord and Founder, and gathered about it we see His

first congregation, pitifully small, yet quite un-
mindful of the shouting mob, the proud priests,
the surly soldiers. That congregation had eyes
only for its Lord and ears that strained to hear
His words alone. Would to God, that might be
said of all congregations named after Christ from
that day to this! Does it not seem to you that the
first church of the cross is a picture of the true
church at all times? There is Christ forever crucified by a sinful world. There are the unthinking
masses, inconstant as the waves of the sea, now
cold and passive, now stormy and raging, driven
they know not why, they know not whither. There
is the impenitent thief, finally caught in his sins
and cursing his lot and his Lord. There is that
other thief, now a new-won member of the church,
saved in the last hour, the man of the last chance,
who seized it and heard the ineffable words, "Today shalt thou be with me in Paradise." There is
Mary, the mother of Christ, the purest and best
of our race and yet not without sin, whose presence in this congregation is evidence as much of
her need of the cross of Christ and its redemptive
power as of human, maternal affection. There is
the other Mary, the sister of the mother of Christ,
the wife of Cleophas, known to us by name only,
but known to God for quiet courage and sweet
secret deeds of loving service. There is a third
Mary, Mary Magdalene, who had lived and suffered under the power of evil until that day when
she met Christ and His word set her free. Now
she stands with undying devotion beneath His

cross, an enduring memorial of Christ's redemptive power and eternal gratitude.

Among these women must we look in vain for
a man? Were there not twelve who swore fealty
to Him in life and death? Where are they? Ah,
there is one. Who may it be? Is it Peter, the man
of vaunted strength of will and purpose, the first
to say that others might fail the captain of their
salvation, but not he? No, it was not Peter. Who
is this lonely disciple beneath the cross? Is it
Thomas who but a short time ago with dogged
determination mingled with self-pity said to all
the disciples, "Let us also go, that we may die
with Him!" No, it was not Thomas. Was it perhaps James who was so sure in other days that
he could drink the Master's cup and he could be
baptized with the Master's baptism? No, it was
not James. Where are they all? Where are the
men? Where are they when the Master's eye
sweeps across the congregation? Peter the proud
is out in the dark, his soul burning with the sting
of a threefold denial. And the others? All have
fled and are scattered like sheep that have no
shepherd. All but one and that one is John, identified not by name but by the telling phrase, "the
disciple whom Jesus loved." Down the ages these
words fly the danger signal to all who seek the
hope of their eternal salvation in their will, their
zeal, their love and their devotion, their good intentions. Down the corridors of time they wing
their way into every honest human heart and

evoke the fervent avowal: Not in us; not in us, O Lord, but in Thy love is our salvation.

That love is wide as eternity, deep as infinity. It is the heartbeat of the Lamb that beareth the sin of the world. It is the blood of the just shed for the unjust. It is life going into the jaws of death, that we, yea, all who are born to die, might live eternally.

Now in this titanic struggle between the power of good and all the powers of evil, the eye of Christ, though rolling in agony, though viewing the welfare of all ages and conditions of men, though about to break in brutal death, beholds that little group of disciples and His mother in the midst. Oh, what sorrow and what comfort their presence spells! Forgotten is the sleepless night and the agony of Gethsemane when the sweat stood like drops of blood upon His brow; forgotten the long anguish of the morning when He was scourged and crowned with thorns; forgotten the taunts and jeers and nameless shame fiends in human forms heaped upon Him; forgotten the horrible thirst, the inconstancy of friends, the ugly betrayal, the pain of quivering nerves and tortured muscles. Aye, forgotten for a moment the onrushing billows of human sin and guilt, the impending doom of Godforsakenness— all this forgotten while His eyes sweep over that little group of the faithful and rest upon His mother. In one quick moment when time seems to stand still as if gripped by eternity, there arise before him, spiritlike, the scenes of His childhood,

the little home back in Nazareth, where faith and
the joys of eternity ruled, even though want and
poverty were daily unbidden guests. He hears
again the sweet voice of mother crooning Him to
sleep with songs reminiscent of angelic anthems
in His heavenly home. He sees her hurrying to
Him with anxious look that day in the temple
when He was twelve, and hears her gentle chid-
ing, "Son, why hast thou thus dealt with us?"
met by His gentle reproof, "Why have ye sought
me? Wist ye not that I must be about my Father's
business?" He relives that day so long ago in
Cana where He wrought His first miracle and her
maternal intrusion in His office and ministry
forced Him to utter a kind but firm reprimand,
"Woman, what have I to do with thee?" He re-
members that later day when again she sought to
intervene and curb His zeal, to dampen the ardor
of His love and to restrict the work of His mercy.
Her messengers approached Him saying, "Thy
mother and thy brothers seek thee." And once
more He had to put her in her proper place, saying, "Who is my mother? and who are my brothers?" And stretching out His hand toward His
disciples He said, "Behold my mother and my
brothers! For whosoever shall do the will of my
Father in heaven, the same is my brother, and
sister, and mother."

And now, there she stands beneath the shameful
cross, so sad and pitiful, so bent and frail, for all
the world to see. But she has not come to increase
His pain but to assure Him and us all that her

faith in Him as the Divine Redeemer of whom the angels sang on Bethlehem's fields is cleansed and strengthened. The sword of which the prophet spoke has pierced her soul, cutting away the last vestiges of sinful, material longings, destroying the dream castles she had built on the shifting sands of vain tradition. In her soul Christ beholds a purified faith in Him, her Son and the Son of God. That is why no heart-rending shrieks come from her lips, neither does she swoon even though her motherly heart be torn with anguish. In this moment the Blessed among women, the humble handmaiden of the Lord, is more than mother to her son; she is an angel ministering to her divine Lord and the words He sees her lips forming must be like these: "Wounded, aye, bitterly wounded, art Thou my Son; but wounded for our transgressions and bruised for our iniquities. The chastisement of our peace is upon Thee and with Thy stripes are we healed." What awful sorrow, what bliss divine meet here!

Then from His cross as from a lofty throne He looks down upon His mother and the disciple whom He loved, considering their every need. Sovereign Ruler of the world, though nailed to the cross, He shapes their future as He wills. He severs the ties that bound them to Him. To His mother He says, mark well, not "Mother"—but "Woman, behold thy son"; to John, "Son, behold thy mother." He gives His mother another son, His friend a new counsellor. For her He provides an earthly home; for John, new duties; while for

Himself there yet remains the loneliness of the cross and the bitterness of vicarious death.

THE FOURTH WORD

My God, my God, why hast thou forsaken me? Matthew 27. 46.

THERE was darkness over all the land from noon till midafternoon on the day when Christ was crucified. He came into the world with light, not with darkness. "I am the light of the world," He said, "he that follows me shall not walk in darkness, but have the light of life." "He came to his own, and they that were his own received him not, but as many as received him, to them he gave the power to become the children of God." They that were His own received Him not. A cross for a deathbed was all that humanity had to offer Him in return for His love. Surely, it was fitting that darkness should fall upon the land, that the sun should hide its face, and that man should tremble before his maker.

But let us for a few moments, as it were, stand at the foot of the cross on which our Saviour died. We have heard His enemies mock Him in His dying hour, but darkness and stillness now prevails for a moment and we hear the cry of anguish from the cross, "My God, my God, why hast thou forsaken me?" It is not man's attitude to Him that is on His mind, for that is now an experience of the past. Even those that were closest to Him,

whom He had selected to be His messengers and
apostles, had failed in the test. One of them betrayed Him, another denied Him, and they all forsook Him and fled. He alone could perfect our
salvation, and He alone must go down into the
deepest depth of suffering to be the propitiation
for our sins.

Forsaken by God! How can we understand
that? We can not understand it. That we, who
by nature are sinful and have forsaken God, deserved to be forsaken by Him, the Holy One, that
might seem reasonable, but He, the Son of God,
who said, "I and the Father are one," that He
should feel Himself forsaken by God, that is beyond our understanding—that is a mystery!

Why are we so prone to take religion lightly?
Should not this word of Christ deeply humiliate
us? Are we worthy of such a love? It was for us
He suffered this, and He did it freely. He said,
"Therefore doth the Father love me, because I lay
down my life that I may take it again. No one
taketh it from me, but I lay it down of myself.
I have power to lay it down and I have power to
take it again. This commandment received I from
my Father."

I do not pretend to be able to explain what
Christ suffered in that hour or how it was possible for Him to be forsaken by God. In Gethsemane in His agony He prayed, "My Father, if
it be possible, let this cup pass away from me:
nevertheless, not as I will, but as thou wilt," but
here He does not use the term Father, but God,

my God. This suggests a different sentiment. It
is the awfulness of sin that He must feel in all its
weight, because He took upon Himself to suffer
in our stead—suffer for our sins. In all its fullness He must experience what man relatively
must experience when he awakens to a sense of
sin, when he comes to realize what it means, as
is writen in Isaiah, "Your iniquities have separated between you and your God, and your sins
have hid his face from you, so that he will not
hear."

O, friends, who are listening in this moment,
take a little time to meditate upon these words.
What would it help you if you had ever so much
of that which the world can give, but have not
peace with God? Your riches will fail, your health
and strength will pass away, your friends are
only for a while; and soon you must take leave
from those that are nearest and dearest to you,
if then you should say, as is written by the
prophet Jeremiah (8. 20), "The harvest is past,
the summer is ended, and we are not saved."
What, if in your dying hour you should cry out
these words, "My God, my God, why has thou forsaken me?"

So great an interest in you did Christ take that
He would descend into this depth of suffering for
your sake, but you go about untouched by His
love. You busy yourself with things which, at
best, are of passing value, while your eternal soul
is starving. You seek pleasure for the moment,
thinking that it will satisfy the longings of your

heart, but some day you will realize that it was like holding an empty cup to the lips of the thirsty one and saying, "Drink!"

There is indeed another side to this matter, which we should not overlook. There is a great consolation and comfort in these words of Christ. It was in our stead He suffered this. He took our sin and shame upon Himself in order that it should not darken our last hour of life in this world. He emptied the bitter cup of terror for us that we might live in happiness and die in peace. So terrible was that moment in Christ's sufferings that Paul afterward wrote, "Christ redeemed us from the curse of the law, having become a curse for us; for it is written: Cursed is every one that hangeth on a tree: that upon the Gentiles might come the blessing of Abraham in Christ Jesus; that we might receive the promise of the Spirit through faith" (Gal. 3. 13, 14).

Therefore we must learn to accept the merit of Christ's suffering in faith. Our own works of righteousness will not prevail before God. To build upon that unto salvation is to build upon sand, but to set our hope on what Christ has done for us is to build on the rock. We must learn to say with Paul, "But far be it from me to glory, save in the cross of our Lord Jesus Christ, through which the world has been crucified unto me, and I unto the world" (Gal. 5. 14). Then we will also say with the same apostle, "For I am not ashamed of the gospel: for it is the power of God unto salvation to every one that believeth;

to the Jew first, and also to the Greek. For therein is revealed a righteousness of God from faith unto faith: as it is written, But the righteous shall live by faith."

THE FIFTH WORD

I thirst. John 19. 28.

BLESSED Lord Jesus! We are assembled at the foot of the cross beneath Thy suffering and dying form. We beg to gaze upon Thee with tear-dimmed eyes; we beg to utter to Thee our stammering gratitude; we beg to offer Thee our cross-branded hearts. Please, we pray, accept us for the sake of Thy saving love and redeeming grace; and may our meditation be to us a participation in Thy suffering, and unto Thee as a glass of cold water to parched lips. Hear us, blessed Lord Jesus. Amen.

Beloved in the Lord:

May I suggest, as a private exercise in Lenten devotion and discipline that we take time to find the words in Holy Scripture which are descriptive of the sufferings of our Lord Jesus Christ.

For an example: if we begin with the prophetic revelation of the suffering Messiah in Isaiah 53, we find such words as wounded, bruised, smitten, stricken, afflicted, oppressed. If we go the Calvary of the Old Testament as portrayed in the 22nd Psalm we have such expressions as forsaken, roaring, despised, scorned, poured out, melted,

dried up. Or if we go into the earthly life of our
Lord, the fulfillment of the Messianic promise, we
see Him persecuted, hated, cast out, rejected,
spat upon, mocked. From thence we may proceed into the apostolic writings, where we find
the interpretation of the sufferings and death of
Christ, and there we shall meet such additional
expressions as humbled, rejected, obedient unto
death, broken, slain, and innumerable others.

As we catalog these and kindred expressions,
we shall have before us a veritable vocabulary of
the sufferings of Christ with all the component
parts of the one all-inclusive word, the crucifixion.
And we shall arrive at a deeper appreciation of
the cost of our redemption and a fuller understanding of the awfulness of sin. For we shall
hear the shrieking cry rolling down the valley
of time from the mob of sinful mortals, the dis-
cord thereof being echoed and re-echoed from the
canyon walls of the successive generations: Crucify Him! Crucify Him! And we shall hear the
thundering condemnation from heaven striking
with lightning force into the pricked and pierced
conscience of man: Ye crucified Him! May we all
fall prostrate before Him with broken hearts and
in contrite spirits with fear and trembling whisper our quivering confession: We crucified the
Lord of Life; I crucified Thee, my Lord and my
Redeemer!

In this vocabulary of sacred agony we come to
the fifth word of our crucified Lord on the cross
of Calvary, "I thirst," a word which in its connec-

tion carries the unfathomable significance of His excruciating pain.

It was not the thirst of the workman, who after a day's labor in the sweat of his brow comes home to be met with lovingkindness and a glass of cool, refreshing drink from the hand of his loved one. It was not the thirst of the traveler, who after a long and dreary sojourn in the wilderness sees an oasis on the horizon a few hours' journey ahead and who knows that a sparkling fountain is awaiting him there. Neither was it the thirst of the shipwrecked in the embrace of the salty waves whose burning thirst eventually is quenched by the merciful wave of unconsciousness. No! This was an unquenchable thirst where not even a drop of water from the hand of Abraham should be afforded him, eternally hellish in its consuming intensity.

It was a physical thirst, indeed. His bleeding and infected wounds from the nails and the thorns, His sprained and torn muscles, His expanded and disjointed frame accelerated His heart action to a state of palpitation beyond endurance and brought His sensory nerves to register an intolerable feverish heat, which caused the pearly sweat upon His brow and the violent gasping for breath and moisture, and His tongue dried up and His lips cracked as He in inarticulate gutterals cried out: "I thirst!" Oh, that we could have extended to Him a glass of cold water, as He would have done it unto us, be we friend or foe!

While we can not minimize His agony of His

physical thirst, yet we must say that that in itself
was only secondary in nature, or a pain reflected
from His ethical thirst, His thirst for truth. He
who is the Truth was in the grasp of tricky deception and cunning falsehood. He who is the
Righteous One was held captive in the poisonous
fangs of lawlessness and unrighteousness. He was
thirsting for holiness, the Holy One, who had become identified with sin and sinners. His thirst
was a spiritual thirst, a thirst for eternal Life.
He who is the Life was hanging helplessly dying
on the cross. He was thirsting for God, God's
own Son who had become Godforsaken and under
God's wrath and condemnation, an eternal thirst
of the One who is forever barred from the fountain of living waters. "I thirst," He cries. We
hear it and sense it, but our hearts are at the
breaking point because of our helplessness in the
face of His hopelessness.

But listen, beloved fellow sinners, we have not
yet touched upon the most gruesome aspect of
His agonizing thirst, and the essential one. We
have only considered the cause of His thirst, and
the cause thereof is sin, and sin in itself is an
unquenchable thirst; we have only been reminded
of the process and effect of His thirst, and the
process thereof is suffering and the consequence
is eternal death, eternal separation from righteousness and true holiness, from life and from
the Giver of all life, from God and His blessed
communion.

But what was the reason for His suffering;

what was the purpose of such agony; why did He have to thirst? Yes, why? Was He not God and One with the Father from eternity; was He not he almighty co-worker in the divine work of creation; did He not have glory with the Father before the foundation of the world; was He not robed in celestial righteousness and crowned with divine holiness from eternity, was He himself not the second person in the Holy Trinity, the eternal Word of Life and Truth? Why should He thirst?

It was a vicarious thirst. It was our thirst which He suffered and endured in our stead; it was the thirst of the sinner for God, the thirst of the mortal for immortality, the thirst of the lost for salvation, and that is our thirst, the thirst of every human soul. We may not be conscious of such agonizing thirst in our life because of the dullness of our ethical and moral senses which are intoxicated by the terrible narcotics of sin. But Christ knows, for He took upon Himself our mortal, sinful nature and it drove Him to Calvary and it nailed Him to the cross, and if it were not for His vicarious atoning sacrifice and His redeeming grace, we should all eternally be without God and without hope, and lost forever.

This thirst of the human heart is in evidence in every human endeavor but in distorted form, and it is hidden in every human motive, but misinformed about the goal, and it is the compelling force in every human ambition, but misguided in its direction. But Christ knows the thirst of every human heart. He suffered the thirst of the outcast and downtrodden for a fellowship which could not be found; He suffered the thirst of the broken-hearted and the misunderstood for sympathy which was not forthcoming. He suffered the thirst of the vile and the wicked for the quenching of a burning conscience which could not be extinguished. He suffered our thirst, for He knows the despair of the doubting mind which can not find the way, he knows the longing of the bewildered for a sure and steadfast hand which is being withheld from Him. He knows the greedy thirst of the selfish and the crooked for pleasures and treasures which never shall be satisfied. He knows what perhaps you do not know, that the innermost thirst of all the godless and ungodly alike is a thirst for God and His righteousness, for life and salvation, which it is humanly impossible to obtain. He knows, for He suffered our unquenchable thirst.

And therefore our suffering Saviour, Jesus Christ, crucified on the cross of Calvary for my sin and in my stead, is thirsting for us to possess us as His own, for He paid the ransom price for us with His blood, the righteous for the unrighteous; and when He, our blessed Saviour, takes our little ones into His saving embrace in the gracious washing of regeneration, where He gives them the forgiveness of sin and eternal life, then His bleeding heart is consoled; and when He leads and guides them by the hand of His blessed Word, then His suffering face shines upon them; and when the estranged sinner hears His call from

It Was for You. 18.

Calvary to come back home, and he returns from his far-off journey in a foreign land, then He embraces the prodigal with His tenderest compassion; and when His children gather about the Lord's table in confession and faith, begging for reassuring grace, then He imparts to us His broken body and shed blood in holy communion, and then His thirsting soul is refreshed as with a glass of cold water.

Therefore and to this end He stands before us with His outstretched pierced hands beckoning sinners like you and me to come unto Him; to come unto the fountain of salvation which flows from Calvary, the river, the streams whereof shall make glad the city of God; to come, every one that thirsteth, and he that has no money—come!

"And the Spirit and the Bride say, Come. And let him that is athirst come, and whosoever will, let him take of the water of life freely."

Blessed Lord Jesus! We thank Thee for Thy vicarious atoning sacrifice on the cross of Calvary for our redemption and eternal salvation.

We thank Thee for the new and living way which Thou hast dedicated for us by Thy blood, through which we have access to the Father.

We thank Thee for the blessed means of grace, the Word and Sacraments, through which we by Thy Holy Spirit become Thy children.

We join in the chorus of old and say from our hearts: As the hart panteth after the waterbrooks, so panteth my soul after Thee, O God; my soul thirsteth for God, yea for the living God!

> Jesus priceless treasure
> Source of purest pleasure
> Truest friend to me.
> Ah, how long I've panted
> And my soul hath fainted
> Thirsting, Lord, for Thee.
> Thine I am, O spotless Lamb,
> I will suffer naught to hide Thee,
> Naught I ask beside Thee!

And now may the peace of God which passeth all understanding guard our hearts and minds in Christ Jesus.   Amen.

THE SIXTH WORD

It is finished. John 19. 30.

IT has been said, that better word was never spoken. This in spite of the fact that it is a tragedy that it should be spoken by the Son of God, dying on the cross.

The life of Jesus is fast coming to an end and death approaching; the suffering and the agony is finished. His life here in the flesh surrounded by misery of every kind and description, meeting and being tempted by evil in every form, in the open filled with mockery, and the hidden and disguised evil using the cloak of friendship, this trying ordeal was finished. He, who had spoken about His Father's will as no one else had dared to speak, had proved He was faithful unto death.

Obedience was not a demand He made upon others, it was His very life to live in it Himself.

Christ came into the world with but one purpose and that was to become the Saviour of mankind. To accomplish this He had to meet everything the world and the devil prepared to use against Him. He did not come for the purpose of suffering, but the suffering became the path to victory. We can not comprehend what it meant to Jesus to live in a world filled with sin. His soul burned in holy wrath at he thought of evil, and it must have been intense suffering to be able to touch its consequences merely by stretching forth His hand, to stand face to face with a humanity left only a wreck of what it had been when it was created in the image of God.

And then, instead of being hailed as the Saviour from sin and death, to be met with distrust, and disbelief, and scorn, and hatred. It must have taken divine love to overcome it all—but what a price to pay in agony. It was to drain the bitter cup to the last drop.

And today. The world over, Jesus seems to be hailed as the Saviour and the Son of God. Perhaps more so at Easter than at any other time. Palm Sunday comes with its waving of branches and the hailing of the Lord. Easter Day people gather by the millions in the open and in the churches to sing His praise. But soon the world is back again in its old mode of living, the branches die and the song grows weak. It does not disappear in hatred as two thousand years ago, but it is slowly being smothered to death in indifference.

On the outside it does not appear so. But it is a fact, nevertheless, in many a so-called Christian life. A great many are not so spiritually awake that they can hate Christ. They are just indifferent. Once in a while they are stirred up a little, but soon they sink back in the same routine and live only for themselves. They are indifferent to the fact that we have a living Christ in our midst inspiring men and giving power to live His life in a world of sin. They are indifferent to the fact that Christ lived and died also for them. They are indifferent to the fact that to have faith in Christ means to live a new life in Him, to live in the same obedience He lived in, to be possessed by the same love He was possessed by.

"If any man will come after me, let him deny himself, and take up his cross, and follow me" (Mt. 16. 24). That is not the spirit of indifference but a faith in Christ even to the point of denying oneself. Such was His faith in man, that He was willing to die for him, and often the only response He receives is indifference to the life He imparts to all following Him.

The apostle writes that our faith is able to overcome the world. But are we really making use of this power in our daily life? A life indifferent to Christ is not making use of that power and it is overcoming neither the world, nor sin, nor death. It is simply sinking deeper and deeper

as a slave of these powers all the time. The enemies of God and man are not the kind that can
be overcome by indifference. They must be met
face to face and overcome in open battle.

Deep in the soul of man we find fear of death.
It seems to be part of our nature. And naturally
so; we were created to live and not to die. And
when facing death, nearly all, even those who
have given very little thought to God before,
know of no one to turn to but Christ. Then they
are willing to trust Him and beg Him as far as
they are able to lead them through what to them
appears to be only darkness. They are willing
to trust Him with their eternal life in spite of
the fact that they may have lived most of or all
of the few years they have spent in this world
entirely without Him.

They try to find comfort in the thought of dying with the one they were not willing to live
with. They are trying to trust in death the same
Lord they were not willing to trust in life. My
friends, if Christ is worth our trust and confidence in death, should He not even more so be
worth our trust and confidence in life?

The foundation of our faith in Christ is not to
be found in all the great miracles He performed
though we love to hear about them and meditate
upon them, and it is not to be found in the great
sermons He preached and which we dearly love,
but it is founded upon the fact that He was faithful unto death and died upon the cross for our
sake.

There is much sadness for us in Good Friday, with the crucifixion, but it is not all sadness and sorrow. Easter became the great day of victory to all Christians because of Good Friday. It seems as though some of our greatest joys have sorrow as their source, out of which they seem to grow and bloom. At the time, the disciples saw only the cross. Later they remembered what was spoken from the cross, and the cross itself became the emblem of Christ. But as we also have been marked with the sign of the cross, we should bear it openly in our lives and let it remind us of the cost of salvation. Centuries ago it was an honor to be a crusader for Christ. Indifference has changed this. The presence of Christ is far from always felt because indifferent men and women desire to go their own ways and lead their own lives and living as they please without regard for the fact that Christ died also for them. The cross does not mean anything to them and Christ can not be their strength and power.

"It is finished." On God's part nothing is left. The rest depends on our faith. If we can talk about one of the words spoken from the cross being outstanding and greater than the rest it is this one. It contains no teaching and no theology, it states a fact. But it is an all-important fact for everyone feeling the burden of sin, for the helpless, for the despairing, for the mourning, for the sinner without peace. There is left only victory over death itself and the revelation of God's mercy and love in His work of bringing salvation to us. When that came, the last uncertainty was removed from the hearts of men. Christianity became a living reality as Christ became the Rock upon which man dared to build his life.

It takes courage and conviction to build on this Rock. But those who take the step have something to live on that is not going to leave them when they are in the greatest need. What a source of peace it is to know that we may thus commend ourselves into God's hand and receive from Him the spiritual strength to live from day to day, growing in His grace.

Then, when our days in this world are over, we may make the words of Jesus ours, because God's work in us is finished. The cross we took up has become our support, and leading us into the eternal life is He who died that He might give life to the dying and salvation to the lost.

THE SEVENTH WORD

Father, into thy hands I commend my spirit. Luke 23. 46.

THESE are the last words from the lips of the dying Saviour, and they show with marvelous clarity how intimately He lived in communion with His heavenly Father. It is impossible to read the Gospel accounts of the life in humiliation of our Lord without sensing the remarkable intimacy with which He lived with the Father. From the very beginning of His earthly ministry it was this consciousness of his oneness with the Father that characterized His every word and deed. Even when He appeared in the temple as a boy of twelve, it was this same consciousness of an intimate communion with the Father that was the basis of His simple question: "Wist ye not that I must be about my Father's business?"

And later, He gave expression to that same intimacy when He said: "The Son can do nothing of himself, but what he seeth the Father do: for what things soever he doeth, these also doeth the son likewise."

His whole life here on earth was lived in daily communion with His Father. When His day had been crowded and the throngs had pressed Him closely, and he withdrew to seek out some lonely hilltop or some desert spot where he might commune in solitude with the Father, it was but the necessary expression of the union that existed between Christ and the Father.

"I and my Father are one." Always that was His consciousness, the reality in which He lived; and so, when He came to His dying hour, He naturally and confidently committed His spirit into the hands of His Father. This prayer of committal was the necessary and natural utterance of His soul. His life was given consciously and purposefully, and now that he had drained the last bitter drops in His cup of suffering, He consciously and purposefully commended His spirit into the hands of the everlasting Father.

In life and in death, His was the quiet assurance
and firm confidence that the Father's hands were
there to receive Him.

And this fervent prayer from the lips of the
dying Redeemer is an assurance to us also that
there are everlasting arms to receive the children
of God; it reaffirms marvelously to our trembling
souls that there is a heavenly Father, who tenderly, lovingly would extend His hands to receive
His children.

In the 31st Psalm the Psalmist had prayed
similarly: "Into thine hand I commit my spirit:
thou hast redeemed me, O Lord God of truth."
And there are countless thousands of men and
women who because of the Saviour's suffering
and death upon the cross have been able to pray
this prayer; for all who trust in the redeeming
grace freely given through Jesus Christ can face
the dark portal of death with this same assurance, and they too, with all the redeemed in
Christ, can say: "Father, I come unto thee. Father, into Thy hands I commend my spirit."

But if a person is to have these words on
his lips and this assurance in his heart in the
hour of death, he must have his life rooted and
grounded in God. In all the scenes of our Saviour's life His heavenly perfections were dis-
played, revealing Him as true God begotten of
the Father from eternity; but he was also true
man. He suffered and endured pain, sorrow, loss,
and, finally, death, even as we must suffer and
endure; but throughout His humiliation He never

lost sight of the heavenly Father. He lived in His nearness. His life was rooted and grounded in God. And life in God is and must be the basis of all personal trust and assurance. It was the basis of the life that Christ lived here on earth, and it must be the basis of the life that you and I live.

The question then arises: How can we live the life in God? How can we know that God is our Father?

The answer is clearly given in God's own inspired word. Paul writing to the Galatians says: "For ye are all the children of God by faith in Christ Jesus."

And in his letter to the Romans the same apostle says: "For ye have not received the spirit of bondage again to fear; but ye have received the spirit of adoption, whereby we cry, Abba, Father. The spirit itself beareth witness with our spirit that we are the children of God."

And in the first chapter of John's Gospel it is written for all to believe and understand that "as many as received Him, to them gave He power to become the sons of God, even to them that believe on His name."

We often hear people speak of the "fatherhood of God," but in many cases they mean something so broad and so sweepingly all-inclusive that God becomes some dim and distant deity who is expected to straighten things out for us when some tragedy sweeps over our lives or some grave need arises, but who otherwise maintains a comfortable aloofness from us. He then becomes merely a deified convenience.

But the testimony of Christ's life and the testimony of God's Word is unmistakably clear. You are the children of God *by faith* in Jesus Christ, not by virtue of your own convenience, nor merely because of the fact that you are human creatures. To them that believe on His name He gave power to become the sons of God. It is not your natural endowment, but a gift pure and simple. You can neither earn it nor deserve it. It is *by faith* that you cry, Abba, Father, and it is *by faith* that you dare pray: "Father, into thy hands I commend my spirit."

But what is this life in God? Where does it have its beginning? God is love, and the life in God begins with the love of God. That is the source, the wellspring of the spiritual life. It begins not with our love for God, nor with the manifestation of our love toward others, but it begins with the love of God toward us. Therein we have the reason for the coming of Christ down to earth; therein lies the reason for His life among men and for His death upon the cross. God loved from the beginning, from all eternity even until now is His love toward us. And His love is in spite of our sin. Sin separates between God and man, but in Christ our Mediator there is forgiveness and access to God. Christ has atoned for our sin upon His cross so that we are free from its guilt and condemnation. Thus a sin-stricken individual finds cleansing and salvation in Jesus

Christ; and God through His spirit kindles a new life, a new spiritual life within our hearts. That is the life in God?

And that life is possible for you, whoever you are and whatever you are; for it is God who worketh in you both to will and to do. From the very moment that you believe in the forgiveness of sin in Christ, He grants you rest and peace, and from that moment your life is in God and you abide in His love. Then you no longer hide and tremble because of your sin and helplessness, but you look up to God and cry: Abba, Father, because then you know that God is indeed your Father and that He tenderly invites you to believe that "He is truly your father and you are truly his child." And then, dear friend, you make a marvelous discovery; you find that now your heart can speak with God in a way never before possible. You have a joyous confidence when you approach His throne of grace; you experience a new bittersweet intimacy when you in daily sorrow for your sins confess them unto Him and pray for pardon, and you own the joyous assurance that in all things He is your heavenly Father and that with childlike simplicity and trust you may bring to Him all your cares and troubles, all your joys and delights, for it is not only the adversities and distresses of life that may be shared with the heavenly Father, but the joys and pleasures as well. And then, as the life in God unfolds itself and you grow in grace and faith and holiness, you make the discovery of the apostle Paul that nothing can separate you from the love of God. "For I am persuaded," he says, "that neither death, nor life, nor angels, nor principalities, nor powers, nor things present, nor things to come, nor height, nor depth, nor any other creature shall be able to separate us from the love of God which is in Christ Jesus our Lord."

This is the ringing confidence of a man who lived the life in God. The confidence that looks unto God in all things, the confidence that knows that nothing, not even death, can separate us from the love of God.

Indeed, the love of God is all that is left to us in the hour of death. Death levels all distinction. The rich, the poor, the famous, the unknown, the strong, the frail, all are the same in death. In death all our dearest possessions and proud distinctions must be left behind. Only the love of God may be retained, all else is stripped from us.

When Christ was crucified, everything was taken from Him. His garments were ruthlessly torn from His back; His friends and followers were for the most part scattered. He was beaten and despised, and it would appear that here was a man most pitifully poor, but death, even the cruel death of crucifixion, could not deprive Him of His Father's love. And when He was ready to give up His spirit, He knew that the loving hands of His Father were waiting to receive Him.

When Stephen, the first martyr, died, he, too, was stripped of everything. Nothing of the things that men ordinarily hold dear was left to him,